IRISH CITIES

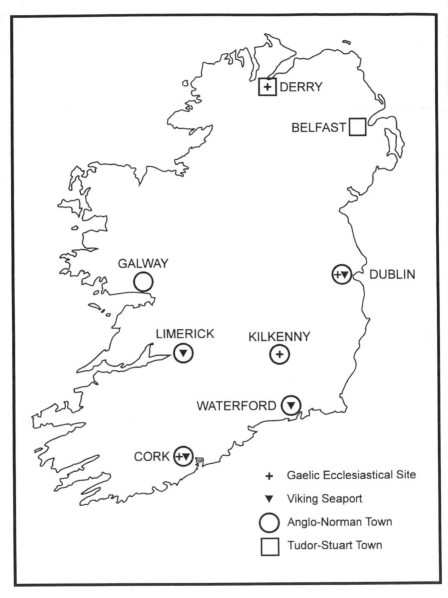

The location and origin of cities included in this book

IRISH CITIES

Edited by

HOWARD B. CLARKE

THE THOMAS DAVIS LECTURE SERIES
General Editor: Michael Littleton

Published in association with
RADIO TELEFÍS ÉIREANN

MERCIER PRESS

Mercier Press
PO Box 5, 5 French Church Street, Cork
16 Hume Street, Dublin 2

ISBN 1 85635 127 0

10 9 8 7 6 5 4 3 2 1

A CIP record for this book is available from the British Library.

Printed in Ireland by Colour Books Ltd.

CONTENTS

Acknowledgements

The editor and publisher would like to thank the following individuals and institutions for their assistance and co-operation: Waterford Corporation for permitting the charter roll representation of that city to be used as the basis of the front cover and in the text, also for the artist's impression by Seán Durack of Waterford; Ciarán Lynch of the Department of Geography, University College, Dublin, for preparing the prefatory location map; Finbar O'Connell for the aerial photograph of Cork; the Trustees of the National Library of Ireland for the engraving of the old custom house in Dublin, also for the photographs of Shandon in Cork and the Claddagh in Galway; DOE Graphics for the aerial photograph of Derry; the Ordnance Survey of Northern Ireland for the map of Derry; Dublinia Limited for the photograph of medieval Dublin; the Ordnance Survey for the basis of the map of modern Dublin [permit no. 6107], also Anngret Simms of the Department of Geography, University College, Dublin, for her constructive comments on Jacinta Prunty's first draft; the Royal Society of Antiquaries of Ireland for the photograph of Georgian houses in Dublin, also for that of the charter roll of Waterford; the Public Record Office, London, for the pictorial map of Galway in 1583; University College, Galway, for the pictorial map of Galway in 1651; Peter Zöller for the photograph of Rothe House in Kilkenny; Limerick Corporation, under whose auspices much of Celie O'Rahilly's excavation and research was conducted, also Patrick Mullins for preparing an up-to-date plan of the medieval city; Trinity College, Dublin, for the pictorial map of Limerick; Eamonn McEneaney of Waterford Corporation for his advice to Terry Barry; Andy Kelly of Kilmacthomas, Co. Waterford, for photography on behalf of Julian Walton; and finally Anne Langheld for retyping many of the edited texts.

LIST OF ILLUSTRATIONS

PREFACE

On 9 March 1995 Queen Elizabeth II conferred city status on Armagh, too late, unfortunately, for it to be included in this series. Armagh had enjoyed city status in an earlier part of its long history, until its municipal corporation, like many others in Ireland, was dissolved under the Municipal Corporations (Ireland) Act of 1840. Long before that again, throughout the Middle Ages, Armagh had been an ecclesiastical city (Latin *civitas*). Medieval writers were notoriously inconsistent in their application of Latin epithets to towns and cities, but there was a long tradition of linking the word *civitas* with the seat (*cathedra*) of a bishop or archbishop. Thereby this usage of medieval churchmen provided a line of cultural transmission back to the late Roman Empire, whose official religion Christianity had become. As Charles Doherty has demonstrated, the idea of a 'city' was imported into Early Christian Ireland with the spirit of *romanitas* itself. The major cult centres, such as Kildare, evolved into ceremonial complexes, in which social differentiation tended to be expressed in purely religious terms. The basic model for such complexes had been established by *c.* 800 and by the tenth century there is evidence of a repertoire of 'public' buildings at the greater monasteries, including Armagh. And thus it was this medieval tradition of elevating focal centres of ecclesiastical organisation that led Stephen Gwynn to incorporate in his book *The Famous Cities of Ireland*, published in 1915, the mere village (as he calls it) of Maynooth.

If the idea of a city goes back a very long way in Irish history, cities as we understand them took centuries to evolve. Behind the English word 'city' lie the Latin words *civis* (citizen) and *civitas* (citizenry, citizenship). In modern usage the word tends to be restricted to the largest and most important urban centres in a country. What ranks as a city varies from one country to another: by world standards most of the cities discussed in this book are rather small places even now and their importance is essentially relative. Down to the nineteenth century the countryside was generally never far removed from city life. Of this the earliest surviving representation of an Irish town or city, that of Waterford *c.* 1370 shown on the front cover, reminds us with its two rabbits outside their burrows in the foreground on the opposite bank of the River Suir.

Ireland's cities have mixed origins. Four were early monastic sites, though none of these evolved into towns without outside intervention – by the Vikings in the case of Cork and Dublin, by the Anglo-Normans in that of Kilkenny, and by the English in that of Derry. These interventions occurred at widely separated dates ranging from the ninth century to the early seventeenth century. Two other Irish cities, Limerick and Waterford, were basically Viking-Age developments on riverine sites. All six cities now situated in the Republic had a formative Anglo-Norman phase in the late twelfth and the thirteenth centuries, during which they acquired the legal status of chartered boroughs and much more besides. On the other hand the medieval urban legacy to Ulster was slight, hence the perceived need to plant new towns in the seventeenth century and the development of Belfast and Derry.

The contributors to this book, as to the corresponding Thomas Davis lecture series broadcast by Radio Telefís Éireann between August and November 1995, have all faced up bravely to a truly daunting challenge – that of telling a coherent story amid so much complexity and often over such long chronologies. They have been encouraged to adopt particular themes, commensurate with their expertise and inclinations, with the result that the emphasis varies a great deal. Amid so much diversity there is not much uniformity, save the compelling and intrinsic interest that every Irish city commands. These essays are illustrative rather than analytical, yet the attentive reader will gain considerable insight into the essence of Irish cities as they evolved in their different ways down to the present day. These complexities go far to explain why none of these places has yet been published in the Royal Irish Academy's *Irish Historic Towns Atlas*. Most of them, however, are under active preparation and Kilkenny, one of Ireland's leading heritage centres, is likely to lead the way. When that happens, a specially commissioned graphic panel will be added to the collection already begun at Dublin Airport as part of Aer Rianta's heritage programme. One fine day, pride of place will go to Dublin itself!

HOWARD B. CLARKE
Department of Medieval History
University College Dublin

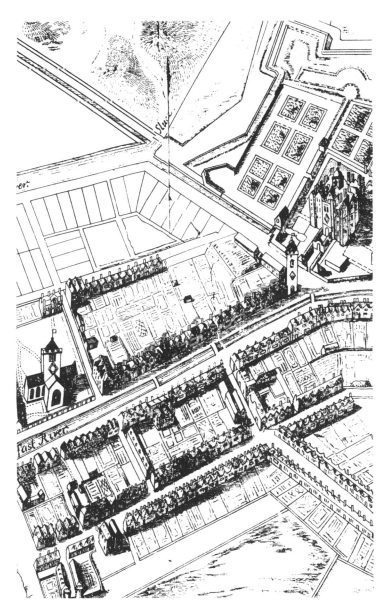

Pictorial map by Thomas Phillips of Belfast in 1685, detail showing the central area. The castle is on the right and the parish church on the left.

14

LANDLORDS AND MERCHANTS: BELFAST 1600–1750

Raymond Gillespie

IN his diary for 1708 the pious Killileagh Presbyterian James Trail recorded the burning of the castle at Belfast. With a morbid fascination he noted how the bodies of three sisters of the third earl of Donegall, the landlord of the town, and one of the servants were carried from the burnt-out shell of the building. Some were unrecognisably burnt while others, the victims of suffocation by smoke, showed hardly a mark. The scene prompted Trail to meditate on the transitoriness of life and how death came to all, from the greatest to the lowest. For those interested in the development of Belfast the scene prompts other thoughts centred on the fate of the Donegall family, landlords of Belfast. It was the second disaster to befall the family in that decade. In 1706 the third earl was killed in Spain while serving with his regiment. The shock of the fire so soon after this tragedy was too much for the dowager countess who left Belfast with her three remaining children, including Arthur, fourth earl of Donegall then aged thirteen, and the family did not return until 1802. The castle was demolished leaving traces only in the street names – Castle Street, Castle Lane and Castle Place.

The abandonment of Belfast by its landlord was an event of considerable significance since it was a landlord town, laid out in the seventeenth century by the Donegalls as part of their estate. In 1500 the site was marked only by a thirteenth-century castle and a chapel, on the site now occupied by St George's Church in High Street. These had been built on a sandbank where the River Farset entered the River Lagan and marked an important ford across the latter. The site attracted considerable interest in the sixteenth century. The castle was refurbished in 1567 and plans were made for a bridge across the Lagan. A settlement in Antrim proposed by the earl of Essex in 1570 included a scheme to erect a corporate town there, but the plans came to nothing.

At the end of the Nine Years War in 1603 the site, along with other land in south Antrim, was granted to Sir Arthur Chichester, a soldier from Devon who later became lord deputy of Ireland. He paid scant attention to the castle of Belfast, establishing his own residence at Carrickfergus where he built a Jacobean mansion at Joymount. The site, however, was regarded as important from a commercial point of view, since in 1604 a grant was made for a Friday market there and in 1608 a fair was added. By 1611 Chichester had begun to reconstruct the castle of Belfast on more fashionable and defensive lines. By the late seventeenth century Thomas Phillips's map shows this as an enclosed five-storey building with a fashionable abundance of gables and a profusion of chimney pots to accommodate the forty hearths on which it paid tax in 1666. The next largest house in the town, that of William Waring the tanner, had a mere four hearths.

In the same year as the reconstruction of the castle began, commissioners surveying the progress of settlement in Antrim and Down noted that a town was 'plotted out', suggesting a formal town plan. Little is known of this plan because the earliest map of Belfast dates from the 1680s and rebuilding during the town's nineteenth-century prosperity obliterated all trace of the pre-1750 town. The fabric of the town was mixed since Chichester used building leases for its construction. This meant that plots of land were set on long leases to individuals

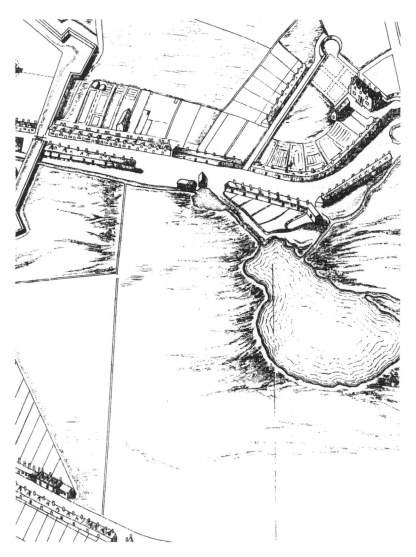

Pictorial map by Thomas Phillips of Belfast in 1685, detail showing part of the suburban area. The gate at the top of High Street is on the left and the mill in the centre. The fortified house on the right was owned by George McCartney, the Belfast merchant.

who undertook to build on the sites. Something of the town's appearance is known from passing comments. Timber was the normal building material. The 1611 commissioners noted that the houses were of good timber with chimneys like those of the Pale. Even chimneys were made of timber, a practice the corporation forbade in 1630. Late seventeenth-century fire-fighting equipment included cuple poles to pull down thatch roofs. There were also brick houses since it was noted that Chichester made enough bricks locally for both castle and town.

It is possible to sketch something of the topography of the early town from surviving leases and the corporation records. As befits a landlord town, much of the early development was around the castle that dominated the town. There was the market-house, where the corporation met, and the market was laid out in Shambles Street, known since 1692 as Corn Market, which lay to the east of the castle. Unlike modern Belfast the axis of the town was not north-south along Royal Avenue, then a narrow street called Harrison's Lane, but east-west from the castle to the Lagan along quays constructed on either side of the River Farset. In 1615 this was known as Great Street, or High Street. By 1667 the inhabitants of this street were responsible for the part of the quays that passed through their property and they were also charged with cleaning the river. The first bridge linking the two sides of the Farset was at Bridge Street, which continued northwards to form North Street and the way to Carrickfergus. Gradually the owners of property on both sides of the river, such as Hugh Eccles in 1664, built bridges wide enough for a carriage. By 1685 a map of the town shows six such bridges across the river. High Street followed the Farset beyond the castle to become the road to Lisburn, but there was little development here until the late seventeenth century. To the north and south of High Street further streets were laid out. To the north lay Broad Street set out by 1617, although built up only in the late seventeenth century by the tanner William Waring whose name it now bears. To the south was Ann Street, again little developed until the eighteenth century. These two streets were linked to High Street by a series of alleyways, or entries as they were later called, such as Skipper Lane and Church Lane.

By 1642 when the town was enclosed by an earthen rampart, still visible into the nineteenth century, its layout was well established. A few smaller lanes, such as Rosemary Lane, which linked Broad Street with Harrison's Lane, had also grown up. The town occupied 86 acres, making it larger than Carrickfergus but smaller than some older east Ulster towns, such as Downpatrick. The existence of the enclosed town was precarious. Problems with fire and disease were never far away. In 1643, for instance, disease ravaged the town. Again in 1689 George Storey, a Williamite army chaplain, recorded passing ten or a dozen corpses in half an hour on the streets of Belfast. The corporation did try to improve urban hygiene. Fines were levied on butchers who left carrion in the streets; they were to bury it in the river at low tide. In 1642 a man was even employed to bury carrion, but such measures had little effect. The Farset was a ready receptacle for household and commercial rubbish and by 1678 its water had become too polluted for even hardy seventeenth-century constitutions. Fire was a major hazard in a timber-built town. The corporation, aware of this, prohibited the building of malt kilns in 1638, and in 1686 required freemen of the town to supply leather buckets and poles for fire-fighting. It was more by chance than planning that Belfast escaped the fires that ravaged contemporary Newry and Lisburn.

The town was vulnerable in other ways. It depended on its rural hinterland for necessities such as turf and food. Townsmen were not cut off from the rural world and many were themselves part of it. Ownership of a plot in the town carried with it land in the town fields. A lease to George McCartney in

19

the 1650s stipulated that half a burgage share in the town fields was 3¼ acres. In 1618 the corporation ordered these plots to be fenced and they were operated as farms. West of the town the River Farset was dammed to form a mill pond at what became known in the early eighteenth century as Mill Street. By 1683 there were four corn mills, one of which had recently been built on the site of an older tuckmill. Belfast also depended to some extent on its rural hinterland for its people. Names on tax lists for the early 1640s, admittedly a time of instability and war, suggest a 50 per cent turnover in people between 1640 and 1642. From the hearth tax lists of 1666 and 1669 one can infer that this is not an unreasonable estimate. These lists also contain the names of a number of native Irish in the town, reflecting migration from the surrounding countryside as well as from England, Scotland and the Isle of Man.

By the 1660s Belfast had become a place of some note, although it still had a restricted range of occupations, mostly butchers, clothiers and merchants. In the 1630s the Dublin merchant, Christopher Lowther, felt it worth having an agent in the town, mainly for the cattle trade, and by the 1660s it was the eighth largest port in the country. The poll-money returns of 1660 record it as the third largest town in Ulster after Derry and Coleraine, although it was poised to overtake the latter. Developments in the mid-seventeenth century encouraged this rapid growth. First, in the 1630s Sir Arthur Chichester's brother and heir, Sir Edward, moved his main residence from Carrrickfergus to Belfast, possibly because of the increasing importance of the town in the family's fortunes. The manor and town of Belfast accounted for over 10 per cent of the family's total rental by the 1630s, rising to almost half by 1719. Graced by the presence of a nobleman, Belfast became a desirable place of residence for the gentry. Increasingly in the late 1630s and 1640s those who became freemen of the town described themselves as 'gentlemen', whereas 'merchant' had been the commonest appellation before. Belfast became a social centre and into the eighteenth century a fortnightly assembly was held in the market-house. This in turn attracted new trades to the town, including by the 1690s goldsmiths and printers. However, it was not entirely gentlemen who were attracted to the town. Merchants, hoping to move in genteel society, gravitated with Chichester from Carrickfergus to Belfast taking their commercial activities with them. By the middle of the century seven-eighths of the customs paid at Carrickfergus related to Belfast's trade. By 1659 Belfast had a customs warehouse and later in the century the Carrickfergus corporation sold the customs rights to Belfast.

While the establishment of the residence of the Chichesters in Belfast was important, there were other factors at work. The strategic location of the town came to the fore in the wars of the 1640s. Belfast became a garrison town. The church and churchyard were fortified until 1656 and the soldiers also occupied the market-house. Later barracks were to be established in Barrack Street. These soldiers introduced new facets into Belfast life, notably their religion – Presbyterianism. This required new churches. A meeting-house was established, according to tradition, first in North Street but quickly moved to Rosemary Lane where it remained into the eighteenth century. The congregation was so large by 1707 that it was divided and a second church was built beside the first. A third congregation was formed beside the other two in 1722, when the original church became Unitarian. The Chichesters, now earls of Donegall, did not see this as an unwelcome development. While they had always adhered to the Established Church, they had strong Puritan tendencies. During the early seventeenth century Belfast had been a Sabbatarian town, with fines imposed for not attending church and prohibitions on selling ale at the time of divine service. During the late seventeenth century successive countesses of Donegall were also sympathetic to dissenting clergy and protected them. It was no accident that the vicar of Belfast, Claudius Gilbert, had been an Independent minister at Limerick during the 1650s. While he conformed to the Established Church at the Restoration, he remained sympathetic to dissenters.

The needs of the people of Belfast in the middle of the seventeenth century were not only spiritual. The presence of a substantial military and civilian population attracted merchants, who saw a ready market for their wares. In the early seventeenth century many merchants who became freemen of Belfast were not residents of the town, needing freedom only to trade. Others, such as George Martin, stayed in the town a short time before acquiring a landed estate. In the 1650s and early 1660s a resident merchant community began to develop and merchants whose names were to dominate the later history of the town appear on the freemen's rolls. In 1656, for instance, George McCartney, later sovereign and leading merchant in the town, was admitted to freedom followed seven years later by the equally influential Thomas Pottinger.

These developments in the middle of the century ensured that Belfast was well placed to take advantage of the dramatic rise in trade that occurred after 1660. Belfast grew from the eighth largest port in Ireland in the 1660s to the fourth by the 1680s. The governor of the Isle of Man, William Sacheveral, believed it to be the second largest port in Ireland by 1702. The volume of butter and beef traded he found almost incredible and indeed the value of its exports in the 1680s was nearly four times that of its nearest Ulster rival, Derry. Much of this prosperity derived from a shift in the nature of Irish trade in the late seventeenth century from live cattle to butter and beef. The Lagan valley, with Belfast at its head, became one of the centres of this trade exporting mainly to England and France. By the 1670s the Belfast merchants had established agents for the butter trade in the towns of the Lagan valley and Belfast became the outport for the growing trade of these towns. As George McCartney wrote to the landlord's agent at Lisburn, George Rawdon, in 1680 in a letter preserved among the State papers: 'if our town [Belfast] prosper, your town of Lisburn certainly must for one depends upon the welfare of the other'. Belfast looked not only west but also built up contacts elsewhere. In 1682 the Long Bridge was constructed at a cost of £12,000 linking the town with the County Down side of the Lagan, a span of 2,562 feet. In the late seventeenth and early eighteenth centuries the freemen of Belfast came not just from the town and its main foreign trading centres but also from Glenavy, Lurgan, Carnmoney, Holywood, Comber, Lisburn and Bangor.

The prosperity associated with the boom in trade showed itself in the physical growth of the town. The corporation expressed its confidence in the new world by leasing a new market-house opposite the castle in 1664 and refurbishing it. Houses appeared on streets hitherto not built up. New buildings on the south side of Castle Street are referred to in 1686 and Waring Street was developed mainly after 1680. It was probably due to this late development that it became the industrial part of the early eighteenth-century town with both tanyards and sugar-boiling works. Thomas Phillips's map of 1685 shows considerable development outside the 1642 rampart, especially the extramural part of North Street, known as Goose Lane, and outside the rampart around the mill. By 1715 these two areas had been joined by George's Lane running parallel to the rampart, but by the 1750s still surrounded by meadows and cornfields. A few of the more prosperous gentry moved out of the town to smarter suburban residences. The Donegalls also made changes in the town with the founding of a school in 1666 in Schoolhouse Lane behind the church.

What is important about this phase of urban growth is that it was not inspired by the Donegalls alone, but rather by a partnership between the landlord and the merchant community. In 1675, for example, a new quay was built at the end of the Farset to accommodate the increase in trade. This was a major undertaking and was still going on in 1681 when four quarrymen were admitted to freedom of the town to carry out the work. On the 1685 map there are indications of improvements being made on the strand. The funds for this development of facilities for trade were provided jointly by the corporation and the Donegalls and they also jointly funded a piped water supply in 1678, the landlords contributing £40 to the total cost of £175. Again in 1672 the Donegalls granted the office of water bailiff to the corporation to ensure that money would be available for the maintenance of the harbour.

It is in this context that the departure of the Donegall family from the town after the fire of 1708 was to prove crucial, for it broke the partnership on which the growth of the town in the later seventeenth century had relied. The absence of landlord leadership and money meant that little was done to develop the town in the early eighteenth century. It was not that there was any lack of ideas as to what had to be done. Maclachan's map of 1715 shows not so much how the town then stood as how it might develop. The area around Smithfield, to the west of the town, still undeveloped by 1757, is shown as heavily built up and around Hanover Quay a never-realised residential development, focused on a 110-foot square called Brunswick Square, was planned. In 1739 the absentee earl of Donegall declared his intention to build a linen hall in Ann Street on the model of that in Dublin and had plans drawn up. Nothing was built, although the site was used for the sale of linens until it was sold in the 1750s. In fact there was only one significant innovation in the early eighteenth century, a private development of two quays, George's Quay and Hanover Quay on the south side of the Farset. This was funded by a merchant, Isaac Macartney, who also succeeded in having the custom house moved there and hoped to recoup his expenditure by charging tolls.

It was not simply the absence of finance provided by the Donegalls that affected the town. By the early eighteenth century the family's fortunes were at such a low ebb that it is doubtful if they could have afforded any significant capital for urban improvement. Rather it was the absence of the leadership that the family exercised in the town which was most apparent. Within a year of the departure of the Donegalls the religious equilibrium of the town, maintained by the family's patronage of both Presbyterianism and the Church of Ireland, was shattered by a pamphlet war between the vicar of Belfast, William Tisdall, and the Presbyterian minister John McBride. In political life, too, the stability provided by the landlord disappeared. From the creation of a corporation in Belfast in 1613 the Chichesters had dominated the political life of the town. The first twelve burgesses and the sovereign had been nominated by Sir Arthur; he appointed their successors and by-laws were made only with the lord's consent. However, the real control over the corporation was financial. Since the town was the landlord's property the corporation had no income of its own and was unable to undertake schemes, such as poor relief, which other corporate towns provided. In 1709, the year after the family left Belfast, the corporation made a bid for financial independence, challenging the right of the Donegall family to collect tolls from ships docking at the quay. The root of the dispute was much deeper, concerning the right of the family to nominate burgesses, choose the sovereign and elect MPs. The corporation were defeated on the issue of tolls by the trustees of the young fourth earl. Lacking any real rationale for their existence in a landlord town, the corporation withered away in the early eighteenth century as the powers of the trustees of the estate increased.

By 1750 the Belfast we have explored was coming to an

end. The following year an application was made to the lord chancellor for a commission of lunacy against the feeble-minded fourth earl of Donegall, then a widower with no sons. Although the application failed, it focused the interest of the trustees of the estate on the town. Leases were about to expire and, unsure of renewals of sufficient length, the owners of buildings had made few improvements. As a result Belfast came to have a rather ramshackle appearance, which was commented on by visitors. Something of the state of the town is indicated by the fact that, according to the hearth money rolls of 1666, there were 204 houses in Belfast. In 1725 Arthur Dobbs estimated the housing stock at 2,093, but by 1757 it had fallen to about 1,800 houses. In 1752 the trustees had a private act of parliament passed to allow them to make new leases of properties in the town. It was the later 1750s before this process began and by then the fourth earl was dead and replaced by a more improving fifth earl. During the remainder of the eighteenth century the town gradually became transformed from its down-at-heel appearance as brick buildings of uniform style, as stipulated in the new leases, were put up. Public buildings – notably an assembly room, a poor-house and a parish church – further enhanced the appearance of the town. Belfast was set fair for its nineteenth-century prosperity.

Select bibliography
J. Bardon: *Belfast: an Illustrated History*, Belfast, 1982.
J. C. Beckett and R. E. Glasscock (eds): *Belfast: the Origin and Growth of an Industrial City*, London, 1967.
G. Benn: *A History of the Town of Belfast*, London, 1877.
[H. Joy]: *Historical Collections relative to the Town of Belfast*, Belfast, 1817.
J. McConnell: *Presbyterianism in Belfast*, Belfast, 1912.

T. G. F. Paterson: 'Belfast in 1738', *Ulster Journal of Archaeology*, 3rd series, ii (1939), pp. 110–12.

P. Roebuck: 'Landlord indebtedness in Ulster in the seventeenth and eighteenth century', in J. M. Goldstrom and L. A. Clarkson (eds), *Irish Population, Economy and Society*, Oxford, 1981, pp. 135–54.

P. Roebuck: 'The Donegall family and the development of Belfast, 1600–1850', in P. Butel and L. M. Cullen (eds), *Cities and Merchants: French and Irish Perspectives on Urban Development 1500–1900*, Dublin, 1986, pp. 125–36.

N. Stevenson: *Belfast before 1820: a Bibliography of Printed Material*, Belfast, 1967.

R. M. Young (ed.): *The Town Book of the Corporation of Belfast 1613–1816*, Belfast, 1892.

THE GROWTH AND DECLINE OF AN INDUSTRIAL CITY: BELFAST FROM 1750

Stephen Royle

IN 1799 George Augustus Chichester became the second marquis of Donegall and inherited Belfast. Three years later he came to live amongst his tenants in what is now Donegall Place in the city centre. He was a popular figure and his name headed many lists of subscribers for charities and social events, though it seems he did not always meet these pledges. This was because his move to Belfast was nothing more than a desperate and unavailing attempt to distance himself from his creditors, though at least he could take comfort from a law that as a peer he was not liable to arrest for debt. He had through prodigality and injudicious investments, many of them at card tables or race-tracks, achieved one of the largest ever personal debts, over £250,000, the equivalent of several million pounds today. This was significant not just for the Chichesters but for the development of Belfast.

George's father, the fifth earl and, from 1791, first marquis, had inherited Belfast and much else besides in 1757 from his simpleton uncle, whose long incumbency had resulted in the near dereliction of the town, as we saw in the last chapter. The first marquis, though an absentee landlord, proved to be an excellent steward of the burgeoning affairs of Belfast. During his period port trade increased, customs revenue being £32,900

Ormeau House, Belfast, 1832.

Hat factory of Messrs John Carmichael & Company, North Street, Belfast c. 1888.

in 1763 and £101,376 by 1795, helped by the instigation in 1785 of the Ballast Board, properly the Corporation for Preserving and Improving the Port and Harbour of Belfast. The roots of Belfast's Victorian industrialisation can be traced to his time. The town's involvement in linen trading increased, the cloth being manufactured in the rural hinterland. Added to the Brown Linen Hall on Donegall Street of 1754 was the austerely elegant, early Georgian White Linen Hall for the trading of bleached cloth, built in Donegall Square on the then southern edge of town in 1785. Shipbuilding developed with William Ritchie's yard being established on the Antrim shore of Belfast Lough in 1791. Textile manufacture, too, began when cotton weaving was introduced as a make-work scheme for inmates of the poor-house. This building, another elegant Georgian edifice of 1774, now Belfast's oldest surviving structure, was on land donated by the first marquis and, befitting his position, he was foremost in donations of land or money for good causes.

Belfast's population grew as its activity increased, from 8,549 in 1757 to 18,320 in 1791. Though many people lived in squalor, especially to the west and in alleys off the principal thoroughfares, others lived well and, thanks to the first marquis, the overall appearance of Belfast was pleasing – it was, after all, the 'Athens of the north'. He laid out new streets and ensured that property built on them was to a set standard by inserting restrictive covenants in building leases. The standards varied with area, but were high near Donegall Square, and Belfast had Georgian terraces to rival Dublin's, though fewer of them. Sadly, unlike in Dublin, few have survived. One of the best extant examples is the Chichester Street offices of solicitors, L'Estrange and Brett, fittingly because Sir Charles Brett is active in protecting Belfast's built heritage.

This prestigious area around the White Linen Hall became the favoured residential address of Belfast's wealthy classes in the early nineteenth century, some moving from the previous high-class area in the old town centre to the north. The wealthy did not remain long. Within a couple of generations, following the example of the Donegall family itself, they suburbanised – fled rather – to escape what Belfast became: the classic Victorian industrial city, an urban form common in Britain, but not found on this scale elsewhere in Ireland. The Donegalls had a role to play in this transformation, though under the second marquis it was based on omission rather than commission. The first marquis was aware of his son's character, but was obliged to leave Belfast to him under a family settlement. Ballymacarrett, however, he could leave in the safer hands of another child, this line taking the Templemore title. Ballymacarrett is the townland at the heart of east Belfast, but was then a distant settlement connected by the Long Bridge across the Lagan. The Templemores' responsible approach to ownership was seen from the late 1840s when it was planned to make Ballymacarrett a model industrial suburb, somewhat on the lines of the later Port Sunlight or Bournville in England. The plan failed, but left a remembrance in the form of the one street developed under it, the wide, straight Templemore Avenue, completely out of character amongst the meaner streets that were built here. For Baron Templemore lost interest, concentrated on holdings elsewhere in Ireland and allowed east Belfast to develop in the way the Donegalls dealt with the rest of the urban area – by selling off leases without controls.

The second marquis of Donegall needed money. His holding of Belfast was like a bank deposit to him, so he cashed it in. In 1822 he raised over £300,000 by granting leases for ever at low rents in return for large sums in cash. These leases, unlike those of his father, contained no restrictions and the purchasers could do as they liked with their land, constrained only by the tardy development of planning regulations. The marquis also literally abandoned the city, leaving for Ormeau in the wilds of the County Down riverside. Here he seems to have spent his money building a mock-Tudor mansion rather than paying bills. On his death in 1844 the debt remaining had actually increased to £400,000 and to clear it the third marquis was obliged to let the encumbered estates court sell the remaining holdings in Belfast and 30,000 acres in County Antrim. The Chichesters' long role in Belfast's development drew to a close. Their final contribution was their last Belfast home, (another) Belfast Castle, a mock-Scottish baronial edifice of 1870, built on Cave Hill overlooking the scene of the family's activities. They now live in south-east Ireland: Belfast Castle is owned by the council and can be hired for wedding receptions; Ormeau, which sadly has lost the mansion, is a park; their estate of Belfast has become unrecognisable.

The lands released by the family provided the space on which industrial Belfast could develop. Initially the major industry was textile manufacture, not at first linen but cotton. From its introduction in the poor-house, cotton manufacture became a factory industry with twenty-one mills by 1826, employing 3,600 people. Many mills were in the west of Belfast using water power provided by streams running off the Antrim plateau, that mountain front which provides Belfast's spectacular setting. Shortly steam engines replaced water power and linen replaced cotton. The former development was in response to technological change; the latter the result of the activities of one of the entrepreneurs who replaced aristocrats as the major actors on the Belfast stage. In 1828, when his cotton factory burnt down, Thomas Mulholland had it rebuilt to produce linen, utilising the latest wet flax process developed in Leeds. He was successful; other manufacturers followed his lead and by 1860 Belfast had thirty-two linen mills and just two processing cotton. The traditional rural domestic linen industry of Ulster was no more.

The other notable side to Belfast's industrialisation was

shipbuilding, not now small yards making wooden boats but the mighty leviathans of Harland and Wolff and Workman Clark. Belfast was not an inevitable site for shipbuilding. This is not the Clyde; there is no mighty river with deep anchorages; the Lagan is shallow and was full of sandbanks. In fact, so poor was the river entry into Belfast that in 1839 the Ballast Board employed an engineer, William Dargan, to dredge a deep-water entrance through the final bend to improve access as part of a programme of harbour works. The resultant spoil was dumped and land arose from the water, forming what became Queen's Island. At first this land was used as a pleasure park; later, with the park relocated to Victoria Park, it became one of the world's greatest industrial sites. This new, flat, easily worked land with direct access into deep, sheltered water was ideal for shipbuilding. One person to realise the potential here was Robert Hickson of the Belfast Iron Works, who diversified into building iron ships on Queen's Island from 1854. He appointed Edward Harland as manager. In 1858 Harland took over the yard and three years later offered his assistant, Gustav Wolff, a partnership. Harland was the shipbuilder; Wolff, despite claiming late in life that his job was to 'smoke the cigars for the firm', was an engineer and manager with the bonus of wealthy family connections. Of particular importance was his uncle, Gustav Schwabe, whose Liverpool-based shipping interests were good customers. The early Belfast shipbuilders, Ritchie's, which had become Alexander McLaine and Sons, was bought out by Harland and Wolff in 1878. A decade earlier, two former employees of Harland and Wolff set up Workman Clark, the 'wee yard', but that was only in comparison with Harland and Wolff which by 1914 was employing 14,000 workers. Thousands more had related jobs outside, in engineering and rope-making, for example. The yards' zenith – Belfast's, too – was around the turn of the century when the two yards were amongst the world's largest shipbuilders, and several times had built the world's biggest ship, culminating, of course, in Harland and Wolff's 46,328-ton *Titanic*, whose loss on her maiden voyage in 1912 had actual and symbolic implications for the fate of the city in which she was built.

More symbolism was in the building of Belfast City Hall, completed in 1906. This white, domed, Baroque Revival building with its grand staircase and marble floors is not of retiring architecture. Its replacement, functionally, of the modest, red-brick town hall of 1871 on Victoria Street and, literally, of the understated architecture of the White Linen Hall on whose site it sits, was a sign of grandiloquent civic self-confidence and prosperity. This was not shared by the poor. Their houses, mainly in the west and inner east of the city, were not good, though most lived in small terraces from the second half of the nineteenth century and not back-to-backs as in Leeds or tenements as in Glasgow or Dublin. Their jobs were ill-paid, arduous and often unhealthy, and it is clear that the minority Catholics had restricted access to the better positions and to certain industries, especially shipbuilding. Resentment at this, together with differing political aspirations between Catholics, who supported home rule for a united Ireland, and Protestants, who wished to remain within the United Kingdom, led to periodic rioting throughout the nineteenth century.

At the turn of the century, however, it seemed that home rule had been put on the back burner; Belfast had become a city in 1888, one with a catalogue of fine public buildings, many by the Lanyons and/or Lynn including the Customs House and Queen's College. The Georgian parish church, St Anne's, had just been replaced by the new cathedral. There were grand commercial buildings, especially Robinson and Cleavers of 1888 in Donegall Square. Belfast was growing more rapidly than any other city in the British Isles as its industries attracted migrants largely from rural Ireland. The population was 75,308 in 1841 and 349,180 in 1901. It had even become bigger than Dublin, until that city expanded its borders. Its industries were secure and prosperous. The Protestant businessmen, who ran the city from their estates and villas in the rich urban sectors of the Malone and Antrim Roads or in outer east Belfast, were doing well. So, then, demolish the archaic White Linen Hall and replace it with a building costing £360,000 – more fitting for Belfast's prosperity!

In Donegall Square, by the resultant City Hall, is the Scottish Providential Institution of 1902 which has external friezes commemorating the sources of Belfast's wealth and pride – shipbuilding, textiles and ropeworks. Close by is a statue of Sir Edward Harland. But also in Donegall Square is statuary symbolising causes of Belfast's decline: the Cenotaph, its losses in war and, perhaps as a result of them, the partition of Ireland; and the *Titanic* memorial, the fall from grace of its shipbuilding industry.

Belfast spent much of the nineteenth century increasing in population, economy, power and importance; the twentieth century, now nearly over, has seen almost precise mirror images. Far from being on the back burner, home rule pressure boiled over. Two events in 1916 were particularly important. Dublin's Easter Rising highlighted the impossibility of continued union between Belfast and Ireland, with the rebellion taking place and being bloodily put down whilst theoretically the United Kingdom of Great Britain and Ireland was at war. The other was the first day of the battle of the Somme with its 5,500 casualties amongst the 36th (Ulster) Division. These were largely from what had been the pro-union, Protestant, paramilitary Ulster Volunteer Force. After this it was politically impossible to force the areas from which these people came into a united Ireland. Partition was inevitable, with Belfast becoming Northern Ireland's capital.

This status has helped the city in economic terms without doubt – there are thousands of jobs involved – architecturally, too, the parliament buildings at Stormont being one of the better developments of the interwar period, closing the vista on its magnificent tree-lined sloping drive. In other ways partition has been problematic for Belfast. People not cheered by being forced, in De Valera's phrase, to 'lie under the heel of the [Protestant] ascendancy in the neighbourhood of Belfast' had particular reason to feel aggrieved. The actions of some of them, and the response by authorities and/or opposing unofficial groups, saw periodic bouts of unrest from the 1920s, culminating in the civil rights movement of the 1960s, which tragically slipped into the Troubles from 1969. There have been thousands of deaths, many in Belfast, together with millions of pounds worth of damage from bombs and fires, and the displacement of thousands of civilians from their homes. Whatever the legal, political and/or moral justifications, whatever the righteousness of the causes, the civil unrest that has accompanied Belfast on its twentieth-century journey has been a disaster in economic and social terms. The social problems are obvious; the economic ones relate to the direct cost of dealing with the situation and the difficulty to which it gave rise with regard to attracting investment into a city that in any case would have needed to seek new forms of employment to update its quintessentially nineteenth-century economy.

For it is clear that, even without the Troubles, Belfast would have struggled in recent decades. The First World War had been beneficial in purely economic terms. The immediate post-war period was, too, as restocking and renewal took place. The 1920s, however, ended in the crash and worldwide recession. Recession is not good for shipbuilders, since fewer goods are transported; the mass migrations from continental Europe eased, so fewer people needed to be carried; transport technology began to change, aeroplanes replacing ships. The output of the shipyards fell dramatically – Harland and Wolff launched 125,952 tons in 1912; only 9,260 tons in 1933, though the yard struggled on. Workman Clark could not and closed in 1935, selling assets to Harland and Wolff. Textiles, too, faced difficult times as traditional markets were lost.

The Second World War and its immediate aftermath saw the economy pick up again. The shipyard launched 194,502 tons in 1943 and in the following year it employed 30,801 workers. As many as 20,000 built aircraft for Shorts, who had moved flying-boat operations to Belfast from Rochester in 1936. However, as before, the people suffered from war and not just on battlefields this time. Belfast's air defences were little more than token and in four air raids in 1941 the city lost about 1,000 residents. In particular the east of the city around the shipyard was badly damaged and many Victorian terraces have inserts from the 1950s replacing bombed-out houses.

The post-war period has not been good to Belfast. Its industries were old fashioned, had had insufficient investment and were becoming uncompetitive. In their magisterial history of Harland and Wolff, Michael Moss and John Hume criticise the final period of the thirty-two-year rule of Sir Frederick Rebbeck as managing director, twenty-nine as chairman, who had 'proved increasingly reluctant to change'. He resigned in 1962, aged 84, leaving a yard that was unable to compete with more modern producers elsewhere. After Rebbeck, the yard had to invest heavily in updated facilities. In the late 1960s, with increasing levels of government support, it constructed the massive Building Dock to specialise in oil tankers and bulk carriers, just in time for the oil price rises of 1974 and the collapse of this market. Though the yard survives and, after having had to be nationalised, is again a private company, Harland and Wolff is not the force it was and now employs just over 2,000 workers. The textile industry, too, has lost thousands of jobs, including those in what proved to be short-lived man-made fibre factories outside Belfast. The Belfast Ropeworks, once the world's largest, has gone; the site was reused by a shopping centre, a fate shared by the city's cigarette factory when Gallahers concentrated production in Ballymena. In almost every manufacturing sector there has been retrenchment and Belfast's manufacturing industry employed in 1991 only 14 per cent of its workforce compared to 40 per cent in 1961. Over this period the proportion in services rose from 50 per cent to 82 per cent. Some entire industries have opened and closed including, most controversially, the De Lorean car plant into which the government had invested tens of millions of pounds. The city's biggest manufactory by far now is the aerospace works of Shorts, another once nationalised, now private company that employs 7,500 people. In recent years some external investment has been attracted and strenuous efforts continue to be made by the authorities, supported by the European Union, to gain more jobs. Unemployment remains high, however, and has been over or near 20 per cent for many years in this isolated city on the edge of Europe.

Belfast's fortunes have not always been helped by planning policies. In the 1960s it was thought that the city was too dominant in Northern Ireland. The famous Matthew Stop Line was drawn, beyond which Belfast could not build and its population and industrial growth were directed elsewhere, especially to the new town of Craigavon. More recently effort has been expended on getting people and business back into Belfast as the population decline since its peak of 443,671 in 1951 reached worrying proportions, only 279,237 living within the city in 1991.

Much of this effort has been in housing and infrastructural investment. Belfast's tardiness in dealing with housing – there was precious little done in the interwar period, for example – may have saved it from the dreadful high-rise blocks of the 1960s, though its major development of this type, the Divis Flats, was as bad as anywhere. The legacy of old housing continued even into the 1980s. Then, however, stung by criticisms that Belfast shared with Naples the notoriety of having the worst housing in Europe, even under a Conservative government that was limiting public expenditure, there was massive redevelopment by the public housing authority, the Northern Ireland Housing Executive.

Now Belfast's opposing factions live often in new houses on either side of the so-called peace-lines, the euphemism for the massive brick and metal barriers that divide the city's segregated ethnic ghettoes. The middle classes, those that have not long ago left the city for the pleasant rurality of areas such as north Down, continue, as always, to live in areas that are segregated not by religion but by that more usual marker, money. The Malone Road remains, as one journalist was wont to put it, a million miles from the Shankill or Falls.

In fact, assuming no direct involvement in the Troubles, existence for Belfast's monied classes has long been good. Housing is cheap, the environment is pleasant, and there is a rich cultural life, particularly after the revival of night-life in that part of the city centre now called the Golden Mile, stimulated by the reopening of the Grand Opera House on Great Victoria Street in 1980. The task now is to try to bring a higher quality of life to more of the city's people. The infrastructure is improving, new rail and road bridges across the Lagan, opening in 1994 and 1995 respectively, being the most obvious signs of progress. The former is Dargan Bridge (after the engineer), the latter Lagan Bridge, both contrasting with the regal associations of other Belfast bridges – Queen Elizabeth, Queen's, Albert and King's – perhaps a mark of new political sensitivity. They cross near to areas being improved by the Laganside Corporation, whose mission is to provide housing and new facilities in run-down areas by the river. A major new hotel is planned; a new concert hall is already under development. Housing is much better than it was, though it will always require continuous investment. Unemployment has been falling recently, even though most of the growth is in services, which goes against the grain in this traditionally manufacturing city. And, after the paramilitary cease-fires of 1994, are the Troubles over? If so, that will be the best present this young city could have on what in 2003 will still be only its 400th birthday.

Select bibliography

J. Bardon: *Belfast: an Illustrated History*, Belfast, 1982.

J. C. Beckett and R. E. Glasscock (eds): *Belfast: the Origin and Growth of an Industrial City*, London, 1967.

J. C. Beckett, *et al*: *Belfast: the Making of the City, 1800–1914*, Belfast, 1983.

C. E. B. Brett: *Buildings of Belfast, 1700–1914*, revised edition, Belfast, 1985.

R. H. Buchanan and B. M. Walker (eds): *Province, City and People: Belfast and its Region*, Antrim, 1987.

P. Doherty (ed.): *Geographical Perspectives on the Belfast Region*, Geographical Society of Ireland Special Publications, No. 5, Newtownabbey, 1990.

E. Jones: *A Social Geography of Belfast*, London, 1960.

W. A. Maguire: *Belfast*, Keele, 1994.

M. Moss and J. R. Hume: *Shipbuilders to the World: 125 Years of Harland and Wolff, Belfast, 1861–1986*, Belfast, 1986.

M. Patten: *Central Belfast: an Historical Gazetteer*, Belfast, 1993.

BELOW SEA-LEVEL IN THE CITY OF CORK

Maurice F. Hurley

OF all the Irish cities with Viking and later medieval origins Cork has a singular distinction – it is largely devoid of medieval buildings. The *Guide to National Monuments* does not list a single site in Cork city, and the few medieval buildings in local government and State care are neither well known, well maintained nor well publicised. The dearth of medieval buildings does not, however, refute Cork's claim to be one of Ireland's oldest cities, for Cork, more than any other city in modern Ireland, retains its medieval street plan largely intact in the contemporary streetscape. Furthermore, below the surface a rich archaeological horizon is well preserved in the waterlogged ground, with many buildings of eighteenth- and nineteenth-century date retaining the names of their medieval predecessors.

In prehistoric times the estuary of the River Lee contained many marshy islands, bounded to the north and south by hills heavily wooded with oak and hazel, while ash and yew thrived on the thin soils above the limestone outcrops. Willow and alder would have flourished on the marsh and river banks. The diverse environments of the harbour area offered a plentiful supply of food to the earliest human settlers. Even in those days trackways and trade routes may have converged in the area where Cork city stands, since the two islands that formed the nucleus of the city probably offered the lowest fording point of the River Lee.

The first historically recorded settlement was the seventh-

Aerial view of Cork from the north-west, with the medieval walled area out-lined. The shape was dictated by the city's island origin. The influence of the walled city and its surrounding waterways has in turn shaped the out-line of modern Cork.

century monastery allegedly founded by St Finbarr. This was probably located on the site of St Finbarr's Cathedral, a nineteenth-century edifice, which is built on the shoulder of the south bank of the river. The natural advantages of the site, providing commanding views of the estuary, undoubtedly influenced Finbarr's choice. The foundation became pre-eminent among Irish monasteries. This is reflected in its elevation to the status of cathedral when the diocese of Cork was created at the synod of Ráith Bressail in 1111.

The extent of the original monastic enclosure can be identified in the layout of the modern property boundaries. A round tower stood within the precinct. A description by a French traveller in 1644 refers to an old tower, 10–12 feet in circumference and over 100 feet high which, at that time, was held to have been built by St Finbarr. During the siege of 1690 the tower was occupied by English troops and is said to have been shaken by Irish gun-fire. It subsequently collapsed in the early eighteenth century. A monastery of these proportions is likely to have been the focal point of a substantial secular settlement and the name Cork or *Corcach*, meaning marshy spot, appears in the Irish annals from the late seventh century onwards.

The monastery was also the focus of much unwelcome attention from outsiders. Cork was plundered and burnt by the Vikings on many occasions in the ninth century. The Vikings were not, however, the sole source of misfortune for St Finbarr's monastery, for in 807, fourteen years before the first recorded Viking raid, the *Annals of Ulster* state that war between the monasteries of Cork and Clonfert resulted in a 'countless slaughter of ecclesiastical men and of the noblest of the *familia* of Cork'. The Viking raids were equally devastating with no less than seven recorded plunderings and burnings in the years between 821 and 1012. The Vikings are likely to have settled in Cork by the tenth century and many of the so-called

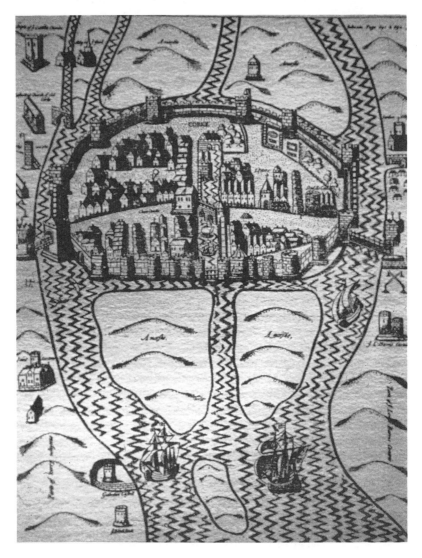

Pictorial map of Cork in 1585–1600.

Viking attacks in that century were not the work of plundering Scandinavians but attacks on an already permanently settled Viking community by other Irish Viking towns in alliance with Gaelic chieftains. The ensuing wars and power struggles clearly show that Viking port towns had become springboards for regional and national supremacy. It was the settled Vikings, more appropriately called the Hiberno-Norse, who through their trading activities established Cork as one of the principal towns.

The primary development of the Viking town was probably on the south island. This reflects the continued importance of the near-by St Finbarr's monastery and the adjacent cove on the south bank where ships could safely be moored. This cove was not infilled until the seventeenth century, but its existence is perpetuated in the name of Cove Street. Documentary sources indicate that this area on the south side of the river continued to be inhabited by the Hiberno-Norse even in post-Norman times, but the topography of a steadily rising slope to the south offered little by way of defence and the south island must clearly be regarded as the core of the Hiberno-Norse town. By the eleventh century the Hiberno-Norse had adopted a standard form of town layout, with one or more main streets fronted by houses with regular property divisions. The initial layout of Cork, from which the modern streetscape is derived, can be traced to Hiberno-Norse origins. There was a single main street, on the line of modern South Main Street, which occupied the highest ground on the central crest of the island.

While the town layout is orthodox, the setting is unusual. The siting of Viking settlements was motivated primarily by defence. Fording points of major rivers and sheltered coves for the berthing of ships must also have been influential factors. Dublin, Wexford and Waterford all offered the ideal combination of conditions, where the defensive site was a high ridge forming a promontory at the confluence of two rivers. This has led to the assumption that it was the high ground that was the primary consideration. The nature of the Cork site flanked by water was, however, equally defensive.

In the absence of hard evidence, the suggested location of the Hiberno-Norse town is based on inference, primarily the evidence of the early Anglo-Norman period. The Anglo-Norman lords, Miles de Cogan and Robert fitz Stephen, besieged Cork in 1177 and this implies that a defended town must already have existed. This must have been on the site subsequently enclosed by stone walls, for there is no documentary evidence for the building of a new town by the Anglo-Normans. Elsewhere in Ireland the initial wave of invaders occupied pre-existing Hiberno-Norse towns, strengthened the fortifications and expelled the more belligerent amongst the Hiberno-Norse or Ostmen inhabitants to near-by locations. It is not until the early thirteenth century that an influx of people was manifested in significant urban expansion.

The medieval walled city remained effectively an island development with its nucleus on the south island. The north island was gradually occupied in the course of the thirteenth century and another long spinal main street developed. The channel between the islands was spanned by a bridge roughly at the junction of Liberty Street and North and South Main Streets today. Bridges at both ends of the town led to the north and south banks of the river. Cork city was succinctly described by Camden in 1568 as being 'of oval shape, surrounded by walls and encompassed and intersected by the river and accessible only by bridges'. The city was about 640 metres long and 220 metres wide. The central waterway provided an enclosed wharf where ships could dock within the safety of the walls. The *Pacata Hibernia* map of about 1585–1600 depicts ships berthed in the area to the south of Castle Street, which formed the north quayside of the dock. A culverted waterway still flows in this channel deep beneath the surface of Liberty Street and the northern side of the Queen's Old Castle shopping mall. The entrance to the harbour was defended by two castles, King's Castle and Queen's Castle, which are romantically depicted on the Cork coat-of-arms. Historical references and maps indicate that King's Castle stood to the south of the channel and Queen's to the north. This is at variance with the perpetuation of the name Queen's Old Castle, which nowadays refers to a building lying largely to the south of the old harbour entrance. No trace of the castles remains above ground, but the rounded gable of the bar known as the Round House at the junction of Castle Street and Grand Parade may be derived from the underlying castle foundations. It is not known for sure when the castles were demolished, but the city court house was rebuilt on the site of King's Castle in 1610.

The plan of the medieval main street is more or less retained in the modern line of North and South Main Streets, though the façades are set further apart. Many laneways leading off the main street at right-angles still exist. Others are fossilised in houses with adjoining doorways to yards and other rear properties. The property ownership of the prominent families of medieval Cork is documented in the names of obscure and now often dismal laneways. Documentary sources and maps identify the names of the lanes – Gallway's, Goold's, Lambley's, Roche's, Skiddy's, Tirry's, Tuckey's and so on – which read like the roll of Cork's mayors down to the early 1700s. Of the medieval families only Skiddy and Tuckey are prominently recorded in the modern street names.

The original paved surfaces of the main street and the lanes are as much as 3 metres below the modern street level. As each generation built new houses above the remains of its predecessor, the ground level rose and the streets and lanes were periodically repaved. The size of the modern property units is, in general, still as it was in medieval times. The units or burgage plots were between 6 and 8 metres wide, with a laneway at the side of each pair of properties. The plots were long and narrow, extending at right-angles all the way from the street front to the city walls. In the thirteenth century substantial timber-framed houses were built and these were probably two-storeyed. Wood was gradually replaced by stone as the principal construction material from the mid-thirteenth century onwards.

Some of the later medieval stone houses, owned by wealthy citizens, were several storeys high and were often described as castles. The buildings are analogous to the tower-house of rural Ireland and as such they are best defined as urban tower-houses. Skiddy's Castle and Paradise Castle, constructed in the mid-fifteenth century, are the best known examples. These so-called castles may not, however, have been significantly different from many of the larger contemporary stone town houses, since the words 'house' and 'castle' appear to have been interchangeable. One account of 1620 states that the buildings in Cork were 'of stone, and built after the Irish forme which is castlewise, and with narrow windows, more for strength than for beauty but they begin to beautify it in better forme'.

Skiddy's Castle was a three- to four-storey structure built in 1445 by John Skiddy, bailiff and later mayor of Cork. Its crenellated battlements must have been a significant landmark, for it is depicted in all the sixteenth- and seventeenth-century pictorial maps of Cork. The castle was owned by various members of the Skiddy and Tirry families; then it passed to the crown and was used as a magazine or munitions store until it was demolished in 1770. The site was the subject of an archaeological investigation in the 1970s and the undercroft or basement levels were found largely intact. Following its temporary reappearance in the mid-twentieth century Skiddy's Castle is again invisible, its site being marked by a bronze plaque. Near by at no. 13, North Main Street a mantelpiece built into the wall above the third-floor window is said to have come from Skiddy's Castle.

Other carved mantelpieces of similar date can be seen in the board-room of Beamish and Crawford Brewery and perhaps the finest of all is that in the Crawford Art Gallery. The latter mantelpiece, dated 1585, is said to have come from the College of Holy Trinity, Christ Church. It is carved with two human figures in costumes reminiscent of those worn by Cork's most famous Elizabethan, the poet Sir Edmund Spenser, who lived in a laneway off North Main Street.

Elsewhere in the city there is a variety of late medieval moulded stonework, often reset in the most unlikely positions in later buildings. A late sixteenth-century window-head is built into a warehouse wall at Wise's Hill. An armorial plaque is set in the wall of the Raven Bar at no. 100, South Main Street; the origin of the plaque is unknown but its present location is close to the site of that other famous tower-house variously referred to as Paradise Castle, 'the Parentiz', or Roche's Castle.

The fate of Skiddy's and Paradise Castles was that of most of Cork's medieval architecture; it has become invisible. Although there are no surviving pre-1700 domestic buildings, many medieval walls and features may lie behind eighteenth- and nineteenth-century façades. Elsewhere substantial amounts of architecture are buried in the tidal levels beneath the streets and houses of today.

The medieval city was surrounded by defensive walls. Standing remains survive in a few places, but extensive lengths have been uncovered in excavations. My own introduction to the archaeology of medieval cities was an excavation in 1981 of the Cork wall at Grand Parade. This was the first time since their demolition in the early eighteenth century that a substantial length of city wall had been visible in Cork. Since then the wall has been exposed in no fewer than ten separate archaeological excavations. In one of these a 60-metre length of wall, with a mural turret and two posterns or private gateways, was uncovered parallel to Kyrl's Quay. These were retained intact beneath the foundations of a new multi-storey car park, but like so much else of medieval Cork they are no longer visible. A short length of wall may be seen beneath the entrance ramp. Another excavated length of city wall is visible at Grand Parade where Cork Corporation retained the structure in a newly created park. It requires a vivid imagination to visualise the wall standing to a height of 3.5 metres and providing secure protection for the inhabitants for over five hundred years.

The building of the city wall was not a single episode of endeavour, and its maintenance was a source of constant concern to the citizens. From the late fourteenth century onwards the walls were in regular need of repair. The principal reason was erosion by tide and floodwaters. One collapse was said to be due to the fact that 'the city is founded on watery soil [and the walls] are daily penetrated by the ebb and flow of the sea'. Today archaeological excavations in Cork are subject to constant flooding and tide charts dictate the work's schedule.

The city walls were provided with additional defensive strength in the form of mural towers and castles. Pairs of castles flanked the north and south gates, and King's and Queen's Castles flanked the quays. Other towers occurred at strategic points. The exact number built or standing at any one time is unclear and the pictorial maps provide contradictory evidence. In all it is likely that there were fourteen mural towers in addition to those flanking the gates. Judging from the walls that survive below ground, the city with its towers, battlements and crenellations must have been a spectacular sight. The mixture of vivid white limestone contrasting with dark sandstone gave a charming mottled effect unique to Cork and is still to be seen on many of the walls of warehouse buildings.

By 1630 the gatehouses were rebuilt as gaols following their destruction by the floods. The gatehouses must have created a very claustrophobic feeling in the main street. In his unflattering description of Cork in 1797 Chevalier de Latocnaye stated that 'the dirt of the streets in the middle of the town is shameful … it would seem as if it were wished to hinder the wind from drying the filth, for the two ends of the street are terminated by prisons which close the way entirely and prevent the air from circulating'.

Two principal churches stood within the walls of the medieval city. Holy Trinity or Christ Church, on the south island, was in existence before 1185. Like other churches of similar dedication in Dublin and Waterford it is probably of Hiberno-Norse origin, but unlike its counterparts it never became a cathedral. This peculiarity undoubtedly relates to the power and special position of St Finbarr's monastery. The present-day Christ Church, now the City Archive, was built in the classical style to the design of Coltsman in 1726. Remains of its Gothic predecessor may have been incorporated into the crypt. St Peter's Church, on the north island, may also be of pre-Norman origin, and like St Peter's in Dublin may have developed from a Gaelic Early Christian monastery.

On looking at a map of medieval Cork, one is struck by the large number of churches and religious houses on the hills to the north and south of the city. Then as now the Cork skyline must have been dominated by towers and spires. The churches of St Nessan, St Michael, St Brigid and St Mary del Nard were probably pre-Norman foundations. The word 'Nard', derived from the Irish *an t-ard* meaning 'the height', is evocative of its location on the ridge above the city where the seventeenth-century star-shaped bastion of Elizabeth Fort now stands. Other parish churches were built by the Anglo-Normans, but their greatest legacy was the foundation of religious houses. In all, five new monasteries and three hospitals were founded in the twelfth and thirteenth centuries.

The Dominican priory was founded by Lord Philip de Barry in 1229 on a previously unoccupied marshy island to the west of the walled city. The name of the priory was St Mary *de Insula*, which clearly refers to its island location. The Franciscan friary was founded a few years later on the north bank of the River Lee, immediately to the west of the north gate, hence the name the North Abbey. These two religious houses appear to have dominated the religious and perhaps also the political scene for much of the medieval period.

The Dominican church was described as magnificent – *magnifica ecclesia*. In 1381 Edmund Mortimer, earl of March and Ulster and father to the heir presumptive of the English throne, came to Cork as lord lieutenant of Ireland and resided in the Dominican priory until his death. It is believed that he was buried within the precincts. After the dissolution in 1541 the priory was granted to a succession of Cork merchants. The Dominicans were re-established for a time in the mid-seventeenth century and in 1689 King James II is recorded as having lodged at St Mary's of the Isle and heard Sunday mass at the North Abbey. It is likely that the division of the king's time between the two prominent religious houses was politically motivated. After 1690 the Dominican priory became the mayor's residence and later it was the town house of the earl of Inchiquin.

When the priory buildings finally disappeared from the landscape is unclear. An archaeological excavation, which preceded the modern buildings now occupying the area, recorded extensive foundations of the priory's domestic range, but the church had fared badly in the site's industrial phase. The recently built student housing complex inadvertently parallels the medieval tradition – a series of cloister-like enclosures housing some of Cork's modern scholars.

In medieval times unenclosed suburbs spread out along

the primary routes leading to the city. The suburb of Shandon occupied the hills rising to the north, while the suburb of 'Faythe' or 'le Fairgh' lay to the south. In post-medieval times and even to this day the residential areas housed a population that daily made its way over North and South Gate Bridges to go about their business in the historic core of the city.

Throughout their history the suburbs bore the brunt of whatever misfortunes befell Cork. They had thrived for a time in the thirteenth century, but the merchants of the walled city used their legal privileges to stifle any commercial competition. In the fourteenth century it is recorded that the suburbs were burnt by 'certain Irish enemies and English rebels'. They lay 'wasted and destroyed' until the seventeenth century. Suburban development is again a feature of late seventeenth-century maps of Cork.

In the aftermath of the so-called Glorious Revolution Cork sided with the Jacobites and was besieged in 1690 by a Williamite army commanded by the earl of Marlborough. The un-enclosed suburbs again suffered badly, this time at the hands of the governor of Cork, who had the suburbs burnt before the arrival of the Williamite army. Following five days bombardment, the walls were breached and the city surrendered. The city walls were probably never again repaired and in 1694 some of the walls were demolished because they were in imminent danger of collapse.

From the late seventeenth century onwards Cork experienced a great economic improvement based largely on the transhipment of provisions to the Americas. The city expanded on every side, the tidal marshes were drained and the city wall was broken down. The economic focus of the city shifted to the newly built streets to the east and this resulted in the survival of the scale, character and layout of the medieval city. This degree of preservation is rarely present in modern city high streets. The unique character of Cork's historic core is now the subject of a long overdue public initiative. St Peter's Church is to become the flagship project of Cork Corporation's endeavours in this regard and it is hoped that medieval Cork can once more, unlike the city described in Paul Durcan's poem, stand proudly above sea-level.

Select bibliography

J. Bradley and A. Halpin: 'The topographical development of Scandinavian and Anglo-Norman Cork', in P. O'Flanagan and C. Buttimer (eds), *Cork: History and Society*, Dublin, 1993, pp. 15–44.

A. Candon: 'The Cork suburb of Dungarvan', *Journal of the Cork Historical and Archaeological Society*, xc (1985), pp. 91–103.

R. Caulfield: *Council Book of the Corporation of Cork*, Guildford, 1876.

M. F. Hurley: 'Excavations of part of the medieval city wall at Grand Parade, Cork', *Journal of the Cork Historical and Archaeological Society*, xc (1985), pp. 65–90.

M. F. Hurley and D. Power: 'The medieval town wall of Cork', *Journal of the Cork Historical and Archaeological Society*, lxxxvi (1981), pp. 1–20.

H. A. Jeffries: 'The history and topography of Viking Cork', *Journal of the Cork Historical and Archaeological Society*, xc (1985), pp. 14–25.

A. F. O'Brien: 'Politics, economy and society: the development of Cork and the south coast region, *c.* 1170 to *c.* 1583', in P. O'Flanagan and C. Buttimer (eds), *Cork: History and Society*, Dublin, 1993, pp. 8–156.

D. O'Sullivan: 'The monastic establishments of medieval Cork', *Journal of the Cork Historical and Archaeological Society*, xlv (1948), pp. 9–18.

W. O'Sullivan: *The Economic History of Cork from the Earliest Times to the Act of Union*, Cork, 1937.

C. Smith: *The Antient and Present State of the City and County of Cork*, 2nd edition, Dublin, 1815.

From the 'Flat o' the City' to the Top of the Hill: Cork since 1700

Maura Cronin

MY father, a Corkman himself, used to say sourly that Cork was built in a hole, as if some malevolent power had stood on an overhanging hill and thrown the place in to find its own level. As an adopted – and therefore more romantic – Corkonian, I prefer to see the city's growth as an upward movement, beginning on what natives call 'the flat of the city', and gradually spanning the River Lee to cover the surrounding slopes.

It was in the eighteenth century that this process of conquering river and hills began. Once the last of the cramping city walls came down in 1703, expansion proceeded at such a pace that by 1750 Cork was described as being 'thrice as large' as twenty-one years previously. The first casualties of this transformation were the river channels which, running like veins through the city, made it similar in every aspect except cleanliness to the typical Dutch town. Firstly bridged, and eventually arched over, these urban waterways had, by the opening years of the nineteenth century, all but vanished. They left no relic behind but incongruous street-names which, though land-locked to this day, include the word 'quay'. Parallel with this went the progressive draining of the marshes to the west and south-east. These advances were both reflected in and accelerated by the establishment of the Wide Street Commissioners who, from 1765 onwards, introduced some element of urban planning into what one uncomplimen-

Shandon and its steeple, Cork, c. 1900.

tary visitor described as 'an old, ugly town'. The limitations imposed by the marshy terrain, the now covered-in waterways and the surrounding hills discouraged the preservation of green spaces. Instead the emphasis was on widening existing streets and on designing new thoroughfares like Patrick Street, the Grand Parade and the South Mall, which were to supplant permanently the old North and South Main Streets as the centre of commerce. Along the growing street network were built imposing town houses for the merchant *élite*, while parish churches like the famous St Ann's Shandon, erected in 1722, rose throughout the city as the ultimate proof of settlement.

But eighteenth-century Cork still had an island mentality. In 1716 it was linked to its suburban hinterland on the northern and southern slopes by several ferries but by only two bridges. The South Gate Bridge linked the island city with the steep and narrow Barrack Street which, in turn, led southwestwards on to the Bandon Road. From the North Gate Bridge ran two equally steep thoroughfares which straggled ever outwards as rudimentary suburbanisation progressed. Shandon Street meandered up to merge with Mallow Lane and descended again to reach eventually the rural areas beyond Blackpool. Blarney Lane turned off Shandon Street at Goulnacpurra and climbed interminably westwards towards Shanakiel before merging into the Blarney road. Not until after 1760 were island and hinterland linked by extra bridges. The most imposing of these was Patrick's Bridge which, from 1789 onwards, joined the newly constructed Patrick Street to the northern slopes. This process of bridge-building continued in fits and starts over the following two centuries, pushed forward by the combined requirements of trade, suburban development, and traffic congestion. By the early 1900s a dozen structures spanned the river's twin channels, while today, following a veritable bridge-building explosion in the 1980s, the total of bridges, small and large, is over two dozen.

It was in the late eighteenth and early nineteenth centuries that Cork's physical expansion went hand in hand with escalating prosperity. Some of that prosperity derived from brewing and distilling. Dotted throughout the old city core and the ever more accessible outlying valleys, the liquor industry owed its initial success to the network of roads that facilitated the transport of grain to the city, and to the abundant water power provided by the Lee and its tributaries. Reverses from 1850 onwards were largely offset by a process of amalgamation, so that by the early twentieth century Cork had become synonymous with Murphy's and Beamish's stout and Paddy whiskey – an ironic position for a city whose best-known public monument, 'the statue', commemorates the nineteenth-century temperance apostle, Father Theobald Mathew.

The most dramatic economic successes were, however, to be found in the northern suburbs around Mallow Lane and Blackpool. Here, from the late 1600s onwards, cattle were slaughtered, pickled and packed for export, the trade employing a multiplicity of butchers, salters and coopers and spawning ancillary manufactures like soap, glue, candle-making and – enjoying a brief comet-like existence in the early nineteenth century – the tanning industry. Small wonder that areas like the Watercourse and Ballymacthomas were smelt before they were seen, one observer in the 1790s commenting on the 'od' rous offal sweets' hanging in the air.

The other great north-side source of Cork's prosperity was the butter trade. Its origins lie in the mid-seventeenth century when, with changes in rural diets and the development of commercial dairying, butter hitherto consumed at home was increasingly sent to market. Country town butter merchants were soon outpaced by the Cork city buyers, canny entrepreneurs who established a constant and guaranteed monopoly through advancing payments to rural suppliers. They also streamlined the regulation of the trade in the city; approved

Map of Cork in 1891.

scales were set up near Mallow Lane to meet the butter coming in from the west and north; prices were standardised; and, with the setting up of the Cork Butter Market under the aegis of the Committee of Merchants in 1769, there was adopted a tight system of quality grading, both of the butter itself and of the firkins or casks in which it was packed. All this gave Cork butter an advantage not only at home but also in the colonies. I suppose the story that a Cork butter firkin was found by Stanley in 'darkest Africa' really was a fiction, but even if it was, it reflected the fact that for 150 years butter and the growth of Cork were synonymous.

As liquor, beef and butter shaped the city from 1750 onwards, so both the fortunes and physical aspect of the hamlets in its immediate hinterland ebbed and flowed with the vagaries of the textile industry. This sector, as in most regions outside Ulster, experienced hard times from the 1820s onwards. The removal of protective duties, lack of capital investment, failure to mechanise, and foreign competition, turned the textile suburbs of Blackpool and the Commons Road, and the outlying villages of Glasheen and Glanmire, into ghosts of their former modest prosperity. Some textile localities survived through adaptation, particularly in the later nineteenth century. By concentrating on the production of high quality woollens, the Mahony family at Blarney and the O'Briens and Morroughs at Douglas ensured that these two communities remained textile-centred as late as the 1970s. Likewise Blackpool remained synonymous with spinning and weaving as the flax factory established there in the 1860s bridged the divide between the old domestic textile trade and successive reincarnations, until Sunbeam finally closed its doors in the 1990s.

From the mid-eighteenth century onwards, such production-cum-distribution provided a ladder to fortune for Cork's entrepreneurs. This, in turn, directly helped to change the shape and extent of the city through suburbanisation. From the

1750s onwards, successful manufacturers and merchants manifested a positive 'passion for country houses' within easy carriage ride of their business places, but removed from the congestion and odours of the city. In this exodus, it was obvious that the local Protestant *élite* was being outpaced by parvenu Catholics, whose large fortunes had been made in areas like Mallow Lane and Barrack Street to be spent from graceful villas dotting the hillsides to the east of the city at Montenotte, Tivoli, Lota and Glanmire and to the south at Monkstown.

That villa building tailed off somewhat in the nineteenth century was indicative of the decceleration of fortune-making in the city. Certainly money was still being made in shipping, railways, food processing and liquor, but the merchant princes of the previous century were gone. Thus when the suburbanisation process accelerated, it was in a less grandiose form, and middle class Cork evolved through linear terrace developments radiating outwards for a distance of between one and three miles from the old city core. Indeed the latter half of the nineteenth century might well be termed the 'age of the terraces'. The number of building contractors increased to capitalise on the growing demand for both quality housing and more modest accommodation. Terraces, graded according to the means and aspirations of intending buyers, crept up the northern slopes and along the main arteries to the south and west where they swallowed up the old peripheral villages. The direction of this expansion kept pace with transport developments. Early in the 1800s, as the growing number of bridges brought new areas within easy walking distance of the city centre, aspiring professionals and business people moved to the terraced gentility of Sunday's Well in the north-west and Wellington Road and Summerhill in the north-east. From 1850 onwards, as six separate railway networks developed in the city, areas like Blackrock to the south-east became popular. Finally, with the establishment of the electric tramway system in 1898, the Western Road, and also Douglas to the south, were drawn into the terraced suburban network.

Along with this outward extension of the city went parallel and somewhat contradictory developments in the central areas. Firstly, from the early eighteenth century onwards, an increased sense of civic pride manifested itself in the already mentioned widening and building of streets and the erection of imposing public buildings from the Corn Market in 1740 to the Cork Savings Bank of a century later. Secondly, as in other urban centres, when the upwardly mobile moved out, so the old core was filled by the poorer classes. Streets formerly the preserve of the merchant *élite* were by the 1830s turned over to minor manufacture and tenement living. The Marsh area around the Mansion House was particularly affected, as were the once genteel Mary Street, Dunbar Street and Cove Street near the South Chapel. Into such places the rural poor flooded during the crisis years of the Famine, so that by 1851 the city's population was 6 per cent higher than it had been ten years previously, and well over half that population lived in slum conditions. The influx (balanced, of course, by emigration) continued less dramatically but no less relentlessly during the successive agricultural depressions of the nineteenth century. In the tenement streets, as well as in the hidden lanes and cabin suburbs, the destitute rented a room, or a corner of a room, adding to the existing misery and overcrowding and – from the ratepayers' cold-blooded but understandable viewpoint – placing an additional burden on the city poor-rate.

The first attempts at improvement had been made in the 1850s when, in order to widen city centre thoroughfares, a number of narrow lanes around Liberty Street had been cleared. As the lanes were levelled, working class eating houses, lodging houses and tenements were demolished, forcing displaced families to move across into neighbouring lanes where they added to the already serious overcrowding. It was not until the 1870s that slum clearance came to be seen as ameliorative rather than cosmetic. The first sign of changing attitudes took the form of a privately owned Improved Dwellings Company. This philanthropic but also profit-making body built a number of small housing schemes on land made available by the corporation adjacent to lane and tenement areas. Later, following a spate of housing and sanitary legislation, the corporation itself became directly involved in slum clearance and the provision of working class housing. Beginning in 1886 with Madden's Buildings in Blackpool, these earliest schemes were built within a short walk of the city centre on former market sites owned by the corporation. Within a few years, however, as the corporation ran out of land and became increasingly concerned by the prevalence of disease in the low-lying areas, sites leased from private individuals and located further away from the core became the norm. By the eve of the First World War, pockets of typical red-bricked housing, which fronted directly on to the street and had a small yard to the rear, were sited half-way up the northern and north-eastern slopes and as far west as the Queen's College. These early schemes certainly played some part in reducing the overcrowding problem. But they were too few in number to meet existing needs, and their rents were considerably higher than those charged for tenement accommodation. Consequently few tenement dwellers moved into them, so that in terms of both population and physical shape, the old medieval core and the hillside lanes remained largely unchanged.

Ironically it was in the mid-nineteenth century, just when the butter and provision trades were declining, that the port of Cork was developed. The harbour was considered one of the finest in the empire, but its inner reaches were inaccessible to vessels of a deep draft, which had to transfer their cargoes to lighters at Passage West for shipment into the city docks. The establishment of the Cork Harbour Commissioners in 1820 began a process of improvement consisting of dredging and jetty-building. This move, speeded up in the 1850s, culminated in the 1870s in the building of the commodious Victoria Wharf on the extreme eastern tip of the island at the confluence of the two branches of the Lee. These developments continued into the twentieth century. Railway sidings were extended to the quays; two new opening bridges were built to facilitate both rail transport and shipping; and further dredging and the erection of additional wooden jetties allowed cross-channel steamers access to the very heart of the city at Patrick's Quay. As the harbour moved into the city, so the city edged down the harbour. Slob reclamation in the 1850s led to the building of the southern Marina embankment, soon to become a popular scenic walk, and behind it the Victoria Park which from 1854 until 1917 was, in turn, an amenity ground and a race-course for the city.

Cork's most dramatic growth occurred in the present century. The commercial centre got a boost from an unexpected quarter in the early 1920s, when compensation for the burning of the city during the Black and Tan presence allowed the rebuilding of much of the eastern side of Patrick Street and the erection of a new and imposing city hall. But the main direction of expansion, dating from the years immediately after the Great War, was down the harbour and over the hills. It was indicative of Cork's declining fortunes that the role played by industry in this expansion was proportionately far less than in the eighteenth century. The butter trade was gone and, though abbatoirs, gut factories and tripe houses still dotted the Fair Hill and Ballymacthomas areas, the north side's day was done. From here on, industry began its slow move down the harbour, beginning in 1917 when the arrival of the Ford Motor Company turned the former Victoria Park into an embryonic industrial zone. Subsequent decades saw the arrival there of Dunlops, Ranks and Gouldings, only the memory of the area's former existence as an amenity park being preserved today in its main thoroughfare's name – Centre Park Road. The reclamation of the Tivoli slobs on the northern bank proved to be tardier. Initially mooted in the 1920s, and begun in the late 1940s, it was finally completed in the late 1960s when the berth for the cross-channel *Inisfallen* was transferred there from what had been known locally as Heartbreak Corner on Penrose Quay. A decade later again, the berth was moved further down the harbour to Ringaskiddy. This coincided with the outward expansion of industrial estates which, from the late 1960s onwards, were located not only on the city outskirts but also as far afield as Little Island and Currabinny, making Cork Harbour one of the main locations of Ireland's chemical industry.

The outward push of residential areas in twentieth-century Cork was much more consistent than that of industry. This arose not only from continuing commitment to the provision of working class housing, but also from the increasing emphasis on town planning highlighted by the Cork Civic Survey of 1926, the Town Planning Act of 1934 and – much later – the first legally-binding city plan adopted by Cork Corporation in 1969. From 1928 and through the 1930s there was an all-out drive to clear the most overcrowded central and north-side lanes. Vast new corporation housing schemes arose on green-field sites, the bus system expanding since 1926 acting as both cause and effect of this new outward push. Thus the northern hills around Gurranabraher became the site of the 'red city' (so named because of its tiled roofs), while other schemes extended over the southern slopes and flatlands at Turner's Cross and Ballyphehane. By the late 1950s, running in tandem with private residential schemes, the encroaching corporation housing moved further south and west engulfing villages like Togher, while in the 1960s and 1970s the wave advanced north-eastwards towards Mayfield, and on to Knocknaheeny in the north-west and Mahon in the south-east.

Today Cork's population, standing at some 135,000, is possibly thirty times what it was in 1700 yet, as one commentator expressed it, the city remains in essence 'a series of small country towns clustered together'. Locality-based loyalties compete and combine with a common sense of 'Cork-ness' epitomised in the lines praising a north-side boxer who 'brought fame to Sweet Fair Hill, and to Cork's own town'. Since the nineteenth century these overlapping loyalties have caused north and south side to face one another in sporting contest between the Glen Rovers and the 'Barrs (or St Finbarr's Club), and in musical competition between the Butter Exchange and Barrack Street Bands. Other inter-locality rivalries are more labyrinthine: ferocious confrontations in the 1930s between football clubs from the environs of Fair Lane and Blackpool could be traced back to the 1890s when the contenders took opposing sides in the Parnellite split, and even further back to vicious faction fights between gangs from the same rival areas in the eighteenth century.

Pride in locality and city has bred a somewhat overweening sense of superiority over the county, summed up in one Barrack Street woman's dismissal of country immigrants as 'bogmen who came in from beyond the lamps years ago with nothing to their feet but cow dung'. Yet, for all that, the underlying nature of the city has always been essentially rural. In the early nineteenth century, for instance, the urban parliamentary constituency included not only the city proper but the surrounding Liberties, stretching out for between five and twelve miles in all directions. Elections thus brought large contingents of country people to the city – some to vote, others to share in the general mayhem of polling day. Moreover the country constantly came to town with the butter carts rumbling in through Blarney Lane and Mallow Lane and with the herds of cattle coming from the railway termini or driven by drovers in the traditional manner. The surviving toll booth at St Luke's Cross in the north-east of the city bears silent testimony to the memory of lowing herds which in my own father's time in the early 1900s wended their way down to the docks, while well into the 1930s cattle heading to the Steam Packet from the agricultural regions north of the city came down through Fair Hill, turning that thoroughfare and the lanes radiating out from it into a medley of confused sounds and pungent smells. Up to the early 1900s, Liberty Street in the flat of the city was the scene of the milk market where farmers gave the traditional tilly for luck. By the 1920s there was still an apple market at the top of Barrack Street and horse fairs were held in the city centre location of Corn Market Street, while during the Emergency of the 1940s grain crops grew in a field beside the Ford Motor Works. As late as the 1960s, when corporation housing schemes and private building moved south and south-west, farming and market gardening were carried on within sight of the advancing buildings, youngsters spending their free hours in the rural hinterland – fishing, hunting, and walking dogs. Even now in the 1990s, the built-up areas stretch no more than four miles from the city centre, so that traditional pastimes maintain the link with the countryside. Bowling, followed with equal intensity only in County Armagh, still takes place today on the same country roads used in the mid-nineteenth century, while drag hunting and pigeon racing have, since the same period, spawned tales of valiant dogs' and birds' derring-do and competitions that cross the divide between country and town.

Like any other settlement shaped over time, Cork's past lies layered within its present. Devotional practices of former times echo through place-names like Sunday's Well and Lady's Well. In the English Market the sale of tripe and drisheen recalls the city's route to short-lived greatness through the eighteenth-century provision trade. Shopping complexes and high-rise car parks stand appropriately on Merchants' Quay and Lavitt's Quay, which commemorate those entrepreneurs who created an island city from a bog. People walk dogs and kick football on green spaces like the Fair Field and Camp Field, where arise the phantoms of herds and regiments long gone. Modern housing schemes spread over areas whose names defy anglicisation – Killeenreendowney, Knocknaheeny, Togher. Above all, in the late twentieth as in the eighteenth century, Cork still maintains the contradictory characteristics dictated by experience and topography. It is shaped by yet suspicious of its rural hinterland; divided yet united by the Lee; and penned in yet drawn outwards by the surrounding hills.

Select bibliography
S. Beecher: *The Story of Cork*, Cork, 1971.
A. Bielenberg: *Cork's Industrial Revolution, 1780–1800: Development or Decline?*, Cork, 1991.
Cork Incorporated Chamber of Commerce and Shipping: *Cork: its Trade and Commerce*, Cork, 1919.
L. M. Cullen and P. Butel (eds): *Cities and Merchants: French and Irish Perspectives on Urban Development 1500–1900*, Dublin, 1986.
S. Dunne (ed.): *The Cork Anthology*, Cork, 1993.
D. Harkness and M. O'Dowd (eds): *The Town in Ireland*, Belfast, 1981.
W. McGrath: *Tram Tracks through Cork*, Cork, 1981.
A. O'Callaghan: *Of Timber, Iron and Stone: a Journey through Time on the Bridges of Cork*, Cork, 1991.
P. O'Flanagan and C. Buttimer (eds): *Cork: History and Society*, Cork, 1993.
C. Rynne: *The Archaeology of Cork City and Harbour from the Earliest Times to Industrialisation*, Cork, 1993.

DERRY –
A SPECTACULAR MAIDEN

Avril Thomas

A THOUSAND years separate Derry Colmcille and London-derry. The new town of 1610 was built at the same site in the Foyle valley as the sixth-century monastic settlement associated with St Columba. Such a long, and sometimes dramatic, history has left a strong imprint on the modern city. Time allows us to look at Derry only in a very selective way, concentrating on a few spectacular aspects which summarise best the essence of the city, both geographically and historically.

'Spectacular' is, surely, the best term to describe the impact presented by a map of Derry, or a view of it from the air. The same is true if the city is approached by sea, through Lough Foyle, or if it is viewed from the high central arch of the new Foyle bridge, also to the north. More often, Derry is approached from the east, either by road or by rail, and then too, the view of the city on the opposite west bank is a splendid one, the more so for the backdrop provided by the mountains of Donegal and Inishowen.

The most striking, and influential, element in Derry's setting is the River Foyle. It has also been its life-line during sieges and a crucial element in its industrial development. The Foyle is a broad river and flows rapidly here in a curving line, rather like an elongated 'S'. The original seventeenth-century Ship Quay was built just outside the town wall at the centre of the bend. Later quay extensions on that side, and railway embankments on the east, have tended to narrow and tame the river alongside the city.

Aerial view of Derry from the south-west.

There was no bridge at Derry until the very end of the eighteenth century. The fine views from the ferry stage on the east bank were not always appreciated by weary travellers. Arthur Young, for example, though a seasoned voyager, noted rather bleakly in his diary for 6 August 1776: 'Reached Derry at night and waited two hours in the dark before the ferry boat came over for me'. Still, as a noted progressive, Young would have applauded the bridge when it was constructed nearly twenty years later, for it was ultra-modern. Known as the Wooden Bridge it was the first of its kind in Ireland. Even more novel, it was largely prefabricated on the other side of the Atlantic. The commission had gone to a Boston firm which had experience of bridging similarly broad, deep and rapid rivers. This may seem unusual but it was as natural for Derry, the trans-Atlantic port, to look there as anywhere in Europe.

This first bridge had great significance, too, because it created a road connection for the first time with the county of Londonderry to the east and made feasible the development of a new area still within sight of the city, the Waterside. The stone Carlisle Bridge replaced it in 1863. It, too, was an innovative development in that it was double-decked. This allowed for a separate road and rail link which, today, takes the form of a double road link.

The Foyle valley is deeply incised at this broad bend, especially on the eastern side where the top, a mere quarter of a mile away, is at over 200 feet. Below this steep slope, the Waterside began as a single street alongside the river, initially to serve the ferry. Its subsequent expansion, after the bridge was built, had of necessity to be along the steep hillside or on the flatter area high above. Perhaps surprisingly, this difficult topography did not prevent virtually a second town arising there during the nineteenth century, with its own commercial core, industries and a range of services such as churches, schools and hospitals. Amongst the first buildings were single residences built by Derry merchants in search of a more spacious grandeur. Later, they were joined by rows of closely packed, brick terraces, the homes of industrial workers. From either, Waterside residents have spectacular views of the Foyle and of the city on the opposite west bank.

That side, too, owes much of its dramatic form to the river. At its centre, Derry is a city set on a hill which has been shaped, not just by the present, but also by an earlier course of the

Ordnance Survey map of Derry in 1904–7, at six inches to one mile.

Foyle. To those approaching from the sea to the north, the site has always looked like an island. Dowcra described it so in 1600, adding graphically that 'it lies in [the] form of a bow bent, whereof the bog is the string and the river the bow'. This is the result of the Foyle taking a more direct course, to the west of a wedge-shaped hill, during the glacial period. The river in time returned to its more easterly, sinuous course, leaving a low-lying, boggy track in its place. In effect, this turned the small ridge at the Foyle bend into an island, isolating it from the higher ground of Creggan, further to the west. Indeed, causeways were needed for permanent routes to north and west Donegal. It was mostly to this area, known suitably as the Bogside, that people from Donegal came in large numbers during the nineteenth century.

The hill or island of Derry, the very heart of the city, lies therefore between a bog on its steep, almost mile-long western side, and a broad river on its slightly less steep, south-eastern and north-eastern sides. Towards the northern end the summit rises to 120 feet, but more than half of its 200 acres are 75 feet above the river or bog. The underlying geology is quite simple – a schist outcrop beneath a layer of glacial deposits. Corn was recorded as growing on the hill in 1600, but the earliest settlers were particularly impressed by its tree cover, and so they called it 'Derry', the oak grove.

As a monastic site, Derry's association with St Columba is well known. He was a local in that he came from the ruling family of the area to the south-west, later known as Tyrconnell. Like countless others in the succeeding centuries, he sailed from the Foyle. His destination in AD 563 was Iona, on the west coast of Scotland, and this serves to illustrate Derry's other important sea link. In fact, this city on the Foyle looks not only north towards the Scottish Islands, but it is almost as close to Glasgow as it is far from Dublin. It is hardly surprising, therefore, if the details of its medieval past, even during its period of monastic prominence, can be glimpsed only occasionally and partially. This is because, although centrally placed within north-west Ulster, Derry was relatively isolated in terms of the whole island. It remained so until the recolonisation of Ulster was planned in the early seventeenth century. Then, the contrast could not be greater from the documentary point of view amongst others. The transformation at Derry from decayed monastic site to new town can be traced most graphically on contemporary maps but, in addition, there are a number of detailed reports. These were commissioned by both the crown and the London companies to evaluate the progress actually being made on the ground, or the lack of it depending on point of view.

One of the most spectacular achievements of the Ulster Plantation was the construction of a formidable town wall at Derry. Incredibly, it was accomplished during just five years, 1613–18. This, and the town laid out within it, was a major exercise in urban planning. It is little wonder that such a costly undertaking was made the responsibility of the city of London, for the government envisaged it as the showpiece of the entire plantation. What is, perhaps, more surprising in an Irish context, and indeed unique, is that both the street pattern and the stone wall have survived almost completely intact. The bastions and curtain wall continue to add emphasis to the hill site as they rise above more recent buildings, and it is also still possible to walk around most of the circuit. The number of gates was almost doubled in later centuries, but this in fact only serves to reinforce the sense of enclosure as one usually enters the heart of the modern city through a gateway. The walls of Derry are one of this island's great historic monuments.

Yet Derry's wall had, like its medieval forebears in Ireland and throughout Europe, a strictly utilitarian purpose – to protect the new town and to provide a refuge in time of need for the smaller settlements around it. Its effectiveness was tested on no fewer than three occasions during the seventeenth century. But even during the last, and most famous, siege in 1689 it was rarely attacked directly. This was largely because it was well guarded and the besiegers lacked suitable equipment. None the less the protection it provided was only partial because, owing to the greater height of the surrounding hills, it was possible to fire cannon balls over the walls. These then fell within the overcrowded streets and houses, causing much death and damage. In addition, on such a restricted site as the island of Derry food was a major problem. The Foyle was, therefore, its life-line, both as a means of supply from London and as a way of escape to Scotland for some of the refugees who had swelled its population to overflowing. When this route was closed by a boom built across a narrow point downstream on the river, the city's isolation was complete. Time was then essentially against it. However, the boom, when tested, proved less strong than it looked, and Derry did not fall – hence the popular name of the Maiden City.

In style that city was designed in a highly regular manner, rather reminiscent of the Roman cities of ancient Europe. This is not surprising because it was influenced by the very latest thinking with regard to town planning which was, itself, classically based. Perhaps the most intriguing aspect is that a layout of such regularity should have been placed, not centrally on the top of the island of Derry, but astride its northern edge. Thus the planned town stretches back from the quay on the Foyle, up the steep northern face of the ridge, and so it has the steepest main street of any major Irish town. The actual line of the wall did, however, lose some of its strict regularity in order to take advantage of slight variations in the detail of the topography. As a result the town plan has a certain lopsidedness to it, being one set of streets broader on the eastern side. From the original gate there, a track led down the hill to the ferry point, for access to the rest of the new county of Londonderry beyond the Foyle. Similarly tracks led south and west from each of the other two landward gates, towards the Donegal countryside. These tracks may all have predated the new town and they long remained the main links with its hinterland.

Within the walled area more than 200 houses were built initially along the four main streets which meet at the central square. There, close to the top of the hill, space was left for a citadel, but a market-house was built instead. This later became the Corporation Hall and, as elsewhere in Ulster, the square itself became known as The Diamond. Today markets are no longer held there, but it remains the focus of the city commercially, despite shops and offices spilling out, as it were, beyond the gates and even into the newer suburbs. City administration moved from the centre, too, when the Guild Hall was built at the end of the nineteenth century just outside Shipquay Gate.

Moving south from The Diamond today, towards the very top of the hill, mainly commercial activity gives way to a more diverse set of functions. The dominant one recalls, visually, Derry's origin as a religious settlement and so maintains a continuity that stretches for nearly a millennium and a half. Derry was built on Church land and, by the time Bishop's Gate is reached, the religious function is still very evident, right across the depth of the city. On the western side the bishop's palace and gardens remain, with a church behind. These all feature on Raven's maps of the developing town, made in the 1620s, along with a school. The bishop later moved out, as did the school, now known as Foyle College. The palace and grounds have been altered and put to other uses, but St Augustine's Church survives rebuilt. It is the most direct successor of Derry's ancient churches because its late medieval predecessor was repaired by the Londoners for use as a parish church. Several decades later a Presbyterian meeting-house was built close by and its successor, too, is still in use.

By 1633 a new cathedral had been built in the opposite, eastern corner of the walls where, being at the top of the hill, it still completes the visual impact of the city. It was dedicated, appropriately, to St Columb and it contains as a memorial a stone from the ruins of the famous medieval cathedral, Templemore, whose site was a little further south down the hill. The fabric of St Columb's Cathedral survives largely intact and so it is Derry's only plantation period building. The grave-yard around it, and the deanery, library and school dating from the eighteenth and nineteenth centuries, add a sense of spaciousness and variety to this part of the walled city. Much of the plantation town was rebuilt in brick during the late eighteenth century. Some fabric of that period survives on the main streets, especially on Shipquay Street, but the minor ones near the cathedral, such as Pump and London Streets, have been less touched by subsequent redevelopment.

South from this area Bishop Street Without continues down the more gentle spine of the hill and a similar diversity is found there too. The Church lands are again the source of this. The first Roman Catholic church to be built at Derry, in 1784, is located close to the site of the original cathedral, Templemore. Near by St Columb's College maintains the age-old educational traditions of monastic Derry. It is built partly on land known as the Bishop's Gardens, where a summer residence called Casino was made for the famous earl-bishop in the late eighteenth century. This was the first prominent house constructed outside the city walls and it started a trend that was later taken up by many Derry citizens.

The nineteenth-century expansion of the city generally was also spectacular, especially in Irish terms. The growth of its population illustrates this most vividly. From approximately 10,000 in 1800 the total expanded rapidly to over 40,000 by the end of the century. The basis of this growth was industrial and commercial development, fuelled by an ever abundant workforce drawn from the surrounding area, especially Donegal. But Derry's westerly location in Ireland was fundamental, too, for once in an advantageous way. Relative ease of accessibility to North America made it the nearest British port to the colonies there. At the same time, its close proximity to western Scotland provided it with a strong link to industrial Britain, in the shape of Glasgow. In addition personal connections strengthened both these contacts. Scots had dominated the population of Londonderry from almost its inception, and it was from the port of Derry that countless emigrants had sailed for America. In the previous century these had included many Presbyterians from the surrounding counties, after the imposition of the Test Act. In fact, settlements had even developed in New Hampshire called Derry and Londonderry.

Inevitably the city's nineteenth-century growth meant that it broke out of its protective shell, the city wall. Porter's map of 1799 shows this process just beginning and the successive maps of the Ordnance Survey trace it in detail. The development of the Waterside began in earnest at this time and, on the city side, many minor streets grew off the original ones leading from the gates. Distinct areas formed, such as The Bogside around Fahan Street, which leads west from Butcher Gate, and The Fountain on the slope below the city wall at the cathedral. New quays were made and reclamation of the Strand to the north-west led to the development of a completely new area, based initially on William Street. This became the focus of an important mixed industrial and residential sector, also with a basically grid layout to its streets. Some streets have survived relatively untouched, for example, Clarendon Street where extremely late Georgian-style architecture still predominates. Other streets have been much modified, particularly those leading up to St Eugene's Cathedral. This is splendidly situated on the edge of the Creggan ridge and it, too, looks down on an area that had a prominent part in Derry's monastic past. Abbey Street still recalls the thirteenth-century Dominican friary. Around its site a distillery and brewing complex developed by the late nineteenth century into the largest of its kind in Ireland. It produced Tyrconnell whiskey whose fame, and flavour, were once well known.

The enterprise of certain individuals was also a crucial factor in Derry's spectacular growth. Amongst the most important of these were John Cooke and William McCorkell, who built up large shipping lines. Their trade was varied and served a wide area of western Ulster. Passenger services in the summer to North America were a major element, as was the import of flax. Sailing ships at the quays on the Foyle are a dominant theme in paintings of nineteenth-century Derry. But, once sail gave way to steam, the locational advantage of being the most westerly major port was lost. Then increasingly ships began to sail past Derry and its brief heyday as a port ceased – but not before Foyle Street, following the curve of the new quays, had become a formidable example of Victorian commercial and industrial development. The arrival of the railways enhanced this process considerably. Indeed Derry was ultimately served by four separate rail companies, each with a quayside terminus.

Today neither ships nor railway stations dominate the Foyle, and many of their associated structures – booking offices, engineering works, mills and warehouses – have disappeared from Foyle Street and the quays. But one of Derry's mid-nineteenth-century industries does retain a prominent presence, and its development was very characteristic of the city. This is shirt-making. Once again the originality of an individual was crucial, as were the dual connections with America and with Scotland. William Scott, a linen merchant, had the idea of producing ready-to-wear shirts for city dwellers, originally with linen fronts on flannel bodies. In 1831 he persuaded his wife and daughters to make some up and, quite naturally, went to Glasgow to market-test them. Success was immediate and its ramifications widespread because there already existed in the domestic linen industry around Derry a skilled, largely female, labour force. American cotton soon proved a better fabric and the sewing machines invented there revolutionised production in time. Much of the resulting factory expansion was made possible with the capital and industrial expertise of Glasgow entrepreneurs. By the end of the century as many as 13,000 people were employed in shirt-making in the Derry area. Unusually 90 per cent of them were women, the men finding employment in agriculture or in the city's transport, engineering and the food-based industries.

The huge, brick-built shirt and collar factories, many of which still survive, were the creation of those who followed William Scott's lead. In them steam-powered machinery was used for both cutting and sewing and the industry was brought right into Derry, instead of being organised from it. Shirt-making has seen many changes since then, but some of its best buildings continue to dominate the city's streets. This they do by their sheer size, rather than as part of a distinct area, although there is a cluster of them on the eastern slope of Derry's hill. Most prominent of all on the steep edge by the bridge is the earliest of them, the Foyle Factory made for Tillie and Henderson in 1856, five storeys high and fronting on to three streets. Just above is Sinclair's four-storey Abercorn Factory of 1863 and, higher up the hill closer to the city wall, is the three-storey factory of Welch Margetson. Built in 1872, with rich detailing in its brick- and stone-work, its eighteen bays stretch the full length of Horace Street. There are others almost within sight to the south and further away to the north-west. The most decorative, the City Factory, still adds interest in the Clarendon Street area.

Shirt-making may be seen as the epitome of Victorian

Derry's spectacular success. The twentieth century has not had such a positive history. Geographical isolation once more came into operation. Unemployment due to industrial decline was compounded by bad housing and by electoral inequalities. These fuelled social strife, endemic in Derry's religious and political diversity. But the Maiden City has always had an instinct for survival, and for revival based on its own resources. Today there is a liveliness about Derry that bodes well for its future. New industries are appearing for which its isolation is irrelevant, its commercial life is burgeoning again and its old centre is being cherished. Few towns in Ireland have as rich a legacy as Derry's – its ancient religious affiliations, its strongly walled centre, its unusual industrial development which produced many substantial buildings suitable for adaptation, and its innovative people – all together in such a spectacular setting on the Foyle.

Select bibliography
T. Colby (ed.): *Ordnance Survey of the County of Londonderry, Memoir of the City and North-West Liberties of Londonderry, Parish of Templemore*, i, Dublin, 1837, reprinted Limavady, 1990.
J. S. Curl: *The Londonderry Plantation, 1609–1914*, Chichester, 1986.
B. Lacy: *Siege City: the Story of Derry and Londonderry*, Belfast, 1990.
P. Macrory: *The Siege of Derry*, Oxford, 1988.
C. D. Milligan: *The Walls of Derry, their Building, Defending and Preserving*, parts 1 and 2, Londonderry, 1948 and 1950.
T. W. Moody: *The Londonderry Plantation*, Belfast, 1939.
T. H. Mullin: *Ulster's Historic City, Derry, Londonderry*, Coleraine, 1986.
A. Rowan: *The Buildings of Ireland: North-West Ulster*, Harmondsworth, 1979.
G. V. Sampson: *Statistical Survey of the County of Londonderry*, Dublin, 1802.
A. Thomas: *The Walled Towns of Ireland*, Dublin, 1992, i, *passim*; ii, pp. 154–62.

Myths, Magic and the Middle Ages: Dublin from its Beginnings to 1577

Howard B. Clarke

THE early history of Dublin, like that of Tara, is associated with a number of myths, the commonest of which perhaps is that the town was founded by the Vikings. The impression has been created that the Vikings came along in their ships, recognised the splendid haven afforded by Dublin Bay, said to themselves 'What a fine spot for a town!' and then set about building one. No thought is given to the fact that, in the ninth century, the people of Norway, whence most of the Irish Vikings came, had no towns of their own, with the possible exception of an important trading settlement called Kaupang located on the western shore of Oslofjord. Kaupang, however, was apparently abandoned quite early in the Viking Age, to become a green-field site and an archaeological treasure-house.

One of the standard myths about Tara has historical implications for Dublin itself. This is the notion that the five great roads of early Ireland radiated from Tara. The latter was indeed a focal point of lesser routeways, but four of the named major routes terminated at Dublin. Three of them probably met at what must be one of the most historic spots in the city, though it is hardly appreciated as such; this is where St Augustine Street, Cornmarket, Francis Street and Thomas

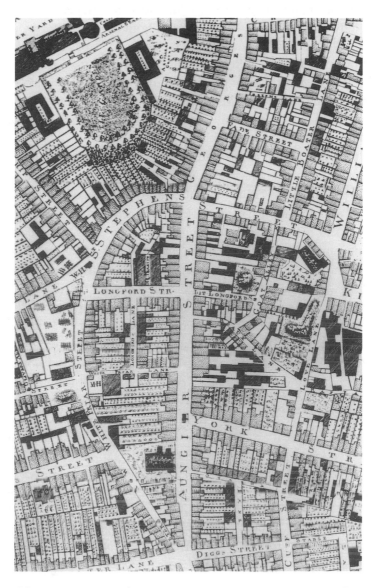

Map by John Rocque of Dublin in 1756, detail showing the outline of the Early Christian monastic enclosure.

Street join together. In order to get to this crossroads, travellers from the north along the Slighe Mhidluachra would have forded the River Liffey at low tide; those from the south by way of the Slighe Chualann would have zigzagged across the boggy lower reaches of the River Poddle; while those from the west would have arrived by way of the great esker trail across central Ireland, the Slighe Mhór. From Early Christian times there seems to have been a wayside church dedicated to St Mo-Lua at this junction and probably long before then a small farming and fishing community had evolved. Conversion to Christianity led to the construction of another early church, dedicated possibly to St Colum Cille (Columba) who died in the year 597 and now represented by old St Audoen's on High Street.

The name of this aboriginal settlement was *Áth Cliath*, meaning something like *Hurdleford* in English, which stood on top of a low ridge running parallel to the south bank of the Liffey. Crossing the Liffey in those days was potentially a hazardous business: in 770 members of a war party from the Boyne valley, having raided successfully in northern Leinster, were drowned in the tideway as they made their way home. From the ridge top in a southerly direction the ground slopes more gently, down to a valley containing a small tributary of the Poddle. Here to this day we find The Coombe, a streetname that means 'valley'. In early historic times this stream would have had a two-fold purpose. One was a source of fresh water for the local inhabitants, for both the Liffey and the lower Poddle were tidal waterways and therefore salty. The other was to carry a fourth long-distance routeway, the Slighe Dhála, towards Dublin from the south-west. Having traversed the Poddle along with the Slighe Chualann near the island site of a possibly early church dedicated to St Patrick, the Slighe Dhála terminated at the eastern end of what we call Bishop Street. Why was that?

The answer to this is the first piece of medieval magic to

Dublin c. 1500.

which I wish to refer. By 'magic' I do not mean the occult, sorcery or witchcraft, but something more akin to conjuring in the sense of conjuring up a surprising phenomenon. The phenomenon in question is an early monastery, whose sanctuary enclosure is still preserved in a pear-shaped pattern of streets in the Aungier Street area. Aungier Street itself was driven across this ancient site in the late seventeenth century, but the earthen bank, ditch or hedge defining the monastic enclosure followed the inside track of Peter Row, Whitefriar Street, Stephen Street Upper and Lower, and Johnson Place – the rest is lost under modern redevelopment. Inside the enclosure there may have been a church dedicated to St Peter, whose parish this was in Anglo-Norman times. Outside the enclosure, to the northwest, a round tower was erected at an unknown date. This monument survived for long enough to be sketched twice in the eighteenth century before being struck by lightning and subsequently demolished.

This was not one of the truly great monastic foundations of early medieval Ireland associated with a famous saint and later with an equally famous school. But the enclosure is a relatively big one and the scattering of church sites of uncertain antiquity includes those dedicated to St Brigit, St Kevin and St Mac Táil – all north Leinster figures. The monastery took its name *Dubhlinn* from an important topographical feature where the castle garden is situated today: a tidal pool scoured out of the Poddle. The last recorded abbot of *Dubhlinn*, Siadal, died in 790, five years before the world as he would have known it was changed irrevocably after the first visitation to Ireland of Scandinavian sea pirates exactly 1,200 years ago. The Age of the Vikings was at hand.

But before we look at that, let us remind ourselves that Dublin already existed as two quite distinct and separate settlements. The one was secular, an informal cluster of dwellings on the ridge top overlooking one of the three notable fords of early historic Ireland; the other was ecclesiastical, a scattering of churches in and around a well-defined enclosure. The names of both settlements, *Áth Cliath* and *Dubhlinn*, are purely Irish and have given rise to the two official names of the modern city, Baile Átha Cliath and Dublin. This dual site had plenty of proto-urban potential, especially when one considers what is likely to have been a prime purpose of long-distance routeways – to enable travellers to embark on ships heading for the neighbouring island of Britain. The fifth routeway, the Slighe Assail, joined up with the Slighe Mhidluachra at Oldbridge, the ancient crossing-place on the River Boyne. The Liffey and the Boyne were the major river systems of what Professor J. H. Andrews has called the 'eastern triangle' of Ireland, whose apex lies somewhere near Mullingar and whose historical significance is particularly marked. The site of Dublin had not only proto-urban possibilities; it had capital city potential as well.

In 837 two great fleets of Viking ships appeared on the Boyne and on the Liffey. In their adventures overseas, many of which were designed for settlement rather than for plunder, the Scandinavians seem to have had an unerring eye for a place to live. Ideal from their point of view was a neck of land between a major river and a side-stream. The neck of land could be defended and the side-stream would provide quiet waters for their ships. The Liffey offered two such possibilities where the Camac and the Poddle approached the main river at a sharp angle, but neither site has yielded unambiguous evidence of ninth-century habitation. What is certain, however, is that the first Viking settlement at Dublin was founded in 841 and lasted until 902. Dublin was not the only Scandinavian settlement in the lower Liffey valley. As early as 867 one of the first Viking kings of Dublin, Olaf the White, had a stronghold at Clondalkin, another monastic site whose round tower has survived. We know this because the annalists recorded the fact that the local Irish burnt the stronghold and then put on display the heads of 100 executed Vikings as a mark of their military prowess.

This brings me to another myth, that of the invincibility of the Vikings in warfare. In the ninth and tenth centuries the Dublin Norsemen lost many more battles with the Irish than they won. In hand-to-hand fighting numbers count and the foreigners must often have been outnumbered by the natives. As the decades went by, the Irish improved their weaponry and even began to use warships, many of them no doubt captured from defeated Vikings. Accordingly the momentous battle of Clontarf, fought with such tenacity all day long on Good Friday 1014, did not put an end to a Viking conquest of Ireland, as the folklore that surrounds that event would have us believe. The fact is that there had never been enough Vikings to conquer Ireland, where marked political decentralisation prevented the Norwegians from emulating the Danes in England. The myth of Clontarf is derived largely from the early twelfth-century O'Brien propaganda tract, *Cogadh Gaedhel re Gallaibh* ('The War of the Scandinavians with the Irish'), but it is significant that the battle occurred near Dublin, for Brian Bóruma's ambition had been to subdue the province of Leinster together with its leading Norse trading settlement.

Again we move from myth to magic. Viking Dublin is redolent with archaeological magic – the revelation before our eyes of a townscape of the tenth and eleventh centuries. Thanks to the labours of many archaeologists, and especially those of Dr Patrick Wallace and his team at Fishamble Street, we now have abundant evidence of the houses, living conditions and daily life of that period. Post-and-wattle houses stood side by side, each in its own fenced enclosure. So uniform in design are the larger types that they must have been built by 'professional' men, who are as likely to have been Irish as Norse. Viking Dublin was not only a hive of economic activity, but also a centre of social interaction. Both Irish and Norse were spoken, intermarriages took place, food and other necessities of life were brought in from the surrounding countryside, and a mixed Hiberno-Norse culture developed. The Scandinavian name for the settlement was *Dyflinn*, clearly derived from that of the old monastic site at *Dubhlinn*.

After the exile of 902–17 the second Viking settlement at Dublin was focused on the Lord Edward Street area, though that thoroughfare is of relatively recent origin. There may have been a quayside at Essex Street West, while Castle Street and Fishamble Street are probably among the oldest city streets. By the second half of the tenth century Viking Dublin had evolved into what might reasonably be called a town. It was the political centre of a Scandinavian kingdom that had a very long history and whose political and legal business was conducted at an open air site. This was the Thingmót on the south side of Dame Street, an artificial, flat-topped mound down by the seashore where kings presided and law-speakers pronounced on difficult points of law. Near by stood the burial-mounds of former kings and heroes that gave rise to the medieval name for this public space, Hoggen Green. Probably in the first half of the eleventh century the earth and timber defences were extended westwards from the eastern core to enclose an area twice as big, including part of ancient *Áth Cliath*. The line of the Slighe Mhór became the east-west spine of the medieval town, following the lip of the natural ridge.

Round about 1030 Christ Church Cathedral was founded jointly by King Sitric Silkbeard and Bishop Dúnán. It stood just below the ridge top, overlooking the Liffey and right in the middle of the enlarged defensive enclosure. Towards the end of the eleventh century the entire circuit of defences was provided with a stone wall, which made Dublin one of the first towns outside the boundaries of the former Roman Empire to have been protected in this way. Other churches were built, including St Michan's on the north side, across the permanent bridge that was erected no later than 1112. Church and bridge suggest a small suburban development, to which a Savigniac monastery was added in 1139. Before long, this establishment was subsumed into the Cistercian order and is known to us as St Mary's Abbey. Soon afterwards that ambitious, energetic and modernising provincial king of Leinster, Diarmait Mac Murchada, was increasing his presence at Dublin by patronising two more monasteries, the nunnery of St Mary de Hogges and All Saints' Priory. Not surprisingly the fortified enclosure (*dún*) of Dublin is described in the *Book of Leinster c.* 1160 as one of the Seven Wonders of Ireland.

Hiberno-Norse Dublin had many of the attributes of a typical high medieval town by the time it was captured by Diarmait and his Anglo-Norman allies in 1170. It did not, however, possess any clearly defined legal status as far as we can tell. There must have been a tradition of collective decision-making by the townspeople, under the presidency of a long line of kings and under-kings, and subject to whatever customary law was generally acknowledged. One of the results of the visit to Ireland of the king of England, Henry II, in 1171-2, when this French-speaking potentate spent much of his time at Dublin in a specially commissioned hall of palatial dimensions, was the granting of a charter. This document was not, as is commonly stated, Dublin's first charter of liberties, at least not in a straightforward sense. It was not even a charter to Dublin or to the people of Dublin. Instead it was a charter addressed to the men of Bristol who were themselves granted the city of Dublin as a place to colonise. What Henry wanted was to build up Dublin into the principal focus of loyalty to the English crown in the new colony. In order to achieve this objective, English merchants and craftsmen were encouraged to settle, with the result that discontented and disloyal Hiberno-Norsemen were banished to the little north-side suburb. This was to acquire the name Ostmantown (later Oxmantown), for the old foreigners were apparently thought of as having come from the east.

Anglo-Norman Dublin after 1170 rapidly became a boom town. The influx of settlers was considerable and there are indications that a population of about 5,000 may have doubled. The existing circuit of walls was elaborated and modified, and gates were inserted or rebuilt. The Winetavern Street opening was called the King's Gate and the thirteenth-century guildhall stood between it and Christ Church Cathedral. A royal castle was located in the south-eastern angle of the Hiberno-Norse walls, the early motte being replaced by an up-to-date courtyard design in the second and third decades of the thirteenth century. The Poddle was rerouted to form a defensive moat for the south wall and for the castle; thus the whole walled enclosure was surrounded by water, except on the western side where the city ditch extended 40 feet wide and up to 19 feet deep. A fresh water supply for the citizens was brought in via an ingenious canal system developed first by the canons of St Thomas's Abbey, a royal foundation dedicated in memory of the recently assassinated archbishop of Canterbury. The Hiberno-Norse walled enclosure was further enlarged by means of reclamation from the Liffey during the course of the thirteenth century.

One of the traditional misimpressions about medieval Dublin is derived from the concept of a walled city. Dublin had its walls, of course, and these were quite substantial. Some parts of them still survive, notably along Cook Street and Little Ship Street. But most of the medieval city lay outside the walls, since extensive suburbanisation occurred in all directions. Each of the four main suburbs had a distinct character. One has already been mentioned, the transpontine suburb of Oxmantown. Its grid plan is indicative of town planning and it had its own triangular market-place outside the north gate of St

Mary's Abbey. A second suburb grew up along Thomas Street and James's Street as far as St James's Church on the way to Kilmainham. This was a typical medieval ribbon development along the main approach road from the hinterland. A back lane towards the north was the pottery-making quarter judging by the name Crockers' Street or Lane. The third example is the ecclesiastical suburb that developed around St Patrick's Cathedral, which had a walled precinct defended later on by tower-houses and containing many other important buildings, including the archbishop's palace. Again this suburb had its own economic focus in the form of a triangular market-place at the northern end of New Street – a thirteenth-century name! Finally there was the recreational suburb of Hoggen Green to the east, where the old Viking Thingmót and royal burial-mounds still stood as mute witnesses to an already ancient past and where medieval Dubliners used to take the air within sight of the sea.

There were other public spaces in the suburbs, notably Oxmantown Green on the north side and St Stephen's Green on the south side. The latter, a bigger expanse than the modern park, took its name from the leper hospital of St Stephen and was used as common pasturage by those citizens who owned animals. Outside the western wall and ditch lay the Fair Green, where every year an international fair of a fortnight's duration was held. Apart from the Augustinian priory attached to Christ Church Cathedral, all of Dublin's monasteries were in the suburbs, tucked away behind their boundary walls and gates. One of the standard myths about medieval monasteries is that all was sweetness and light inside them. On the contrary medieval monks and nuns often found their profession of poverty, chastity and especially obedience irksome, not to mention the sheer boredom of the daily, and nightly, round of chant and prayer. Renegade monks, and even the occasional renegade nun, were quite a common phenomenon, while a rather extreme but by no means exceptional outbreak of disobedience occurred at Holy Trinity Friary in 1379. The story involves the violent death of one of the friars, an Englishman, and the concealment of his body down an unsuspecting citizen's well, before it was returned to the monastery for secret burial.

The period after the arrival of the Black Death in these islands in 1348 seems to have been particularly stressful, to judge by this monastic evidence and much more besides. Dublin was afflicted like most substantial towns and cities in Europe, losing perhaps half of its inhabitants; the city's population may have slumped to 5,000 or 6,000 by the end of the fourteenth century. Morphologically, however, late medieval Dublin remained much as before, apart from the large number of extramural gates erected in the vulnerable suburbs and first documented in the fifteenth century. We hear about constables and watchmen, compulsory archery practice, military guilds, and attempted expulsions of Irish residents. Gates and mural towers were leased to citizens at low rents, with stipulations for their upkeep and for gate-keeping. Such was the degree of paranoia in the second half of the fifteenth century that the Dubliners fell under the spell of the house of Kildare and participated in Yorkist scheming to deprive Henry Tudor of his newly won throne.

To get an accurate idea of what Dublin looked like at that time, may I recommend a little bit of modern magic? At Dublinia, the visitor centre adjacent to Christ Church Cathedral, you can see, among many authentic recreations of medieval life, a scale model of the city including its suburbs. The multilingual commentary gives a brief outline of the city's morphological development between 1170 and 1540, the sites in question being highlighted automatically one by one. At the mention of the Black Death the model city is bathed in a sickly greenish hue and the suburbs are depicted in a partly depopulated condition. The city walls show signs of dilapidation, just as the documents suggest. A photograph of the same model, incidentally, can be seen in the main terminal building at Dublin Airport, thanks to Aer Rianta's enlightened heritage programme. There the illusion is created of looking northwards over the late medieval city as if from an aeroplane, with St Patrick's in the foreground.

A generation later, in the 1530s, Dublin was convulsed by great events propelled mainly by outside forces. In 1534 the citizens petitioned King Henry VIII for six small cannons, one for each of the principal gates: a new age of military technology was dawning. Cannons were used by the forces of Silken Thomas in the rebellion of that year, though both castle and city held out against him. One of the accidental consequences of the rebellion was the brutal murder of Archbishop John Alen, an enemy of the Fitzgeralds who tried to escape from the city by sea, only to be washed up on the shore at Artane. The new archbishop, George Browne, was the king's appointee and he it was, after some hesitation, who ordered the public burning of the medieval relics of Christ Church Cathedral in 1538. The dissolution of the monasteries soon followed and therewith the decisive beginning of the long process of ruination of the medieval city, which has continued down to the present day.

Amid this sombre historical prospect, magic intrudes once more, this time in the verve and vitality of the first extensive commentator on Dublin whose words have survived, Richard Stanihurst. However biased in favour of his native city he may have been, his comments published in 1577 in Raphael Holinshed's *Chronicles of England, Scotland and Ireland* are a revelation. So much of what Stanihurst has to say can be confirmed by other evidence, especially the names of streets, churches and other institutions. Stanihurst's words are those of a young man who was still in his twenties when they were penned;

they reflect the ebullience of youth contemplating an ancient city. By 1577 the myths and the magic of the Middle Ages had been put firmly into the past while yet remaining in the present; they had become in effect history.

Select bibliography
J. H. Andrews: 'The oldest map of Dublin', *Proceedings of the Royal Irish Academy*, lxxxiii C (1983), pp. 205–37.

J. Bradley: 'The topographical development of Scandinavian Dublin', in F. H. A. Aalen and K. Whelan (eds), *Dublin City and County: from Prehistory to Present*, Dublin, 1992, pp. 43–56.

H. B. Clarke: *Dublin c. 840 to c. 1540: the Medieval Town in the Modern City*, Dublin, 1978 [Ordnance Survey map].

H. B. Clarke: 'The mapping of medieval Dublin: a case-study in thematic cartography', in H. B. Clarke and A. Simms (eds), *The Comparative History of Urban Origins in Non-Roman Europe*, Oxford, 1985, ii, pp. 617–43.

H. B. Clarke: 'Gaelic, Viking and Hiberno-Norse Dublin', in A. Cosgrove (ed.), *Dublin through the Ages*, Dublin, 1988, pp. 4–24.

H. B. Clarke (ed.): *Medieval Dublin*, 2 vols, Dublin, 1990.

C. Lennon: *Richard Stanihurst the Dubliner, 1547–1618*, Dublin, 1981.

J. Lydon: 'The medieval city', in A. Cosgrove (ed.), *Dublin through the Ages*, Dublin, 1988, pp. 25–45.

A. Simms: 'Medieval Dublin: a topographical analysis', *Irish Geography*, xii (1979), pp. 25–41.

P. F. Wallace: *The Viking-Age Buildings of Dublin*, 2 parts, Dublin, 1992.

P. F. Wallace and R. Ó Floinn: *Dublin 1000: Discovery and Excavation in Dublin, 1842–1981*, Dublin, 1988.

A Story of Growth and Change: Dublin 1560–1800

Louis Cullen

DUBLIN we know quite well in its role as a Georgian city, or as a Victorian city, or later as the capital of the Irish Free State. The earlier Dublin, from the middle of the sixteenth century to the eve of the Georgian Age, we know less well. We are not even sure of one of its most basic features – what its population was. All we know for certain is that visitors were not impressed by the city, and found it to fall short of the major cities of neighbouring Britain. That view later visitors revised; they began to speak well of it. So we can conclude impressionistically that it was an unimpressive city on either side of 1600 and that the growth, which later began to impress observers, became significant only after that date. That growth in turn laid the basis of the Georgian city, which was admired at the time and later, and whose surviving buildings we now rightly try to protect.

We can in some desperation attempt to calculate the city's population about 1610 from the pictorial map devised by John Speed. It depicts some 900 houses, roughly 600 without the walls, 300 within the walls. If we assumed that each house had six inhabitants on average, that would give a population of just above 5,000 inhabitants. It has, however, been observed that reliance on John Speed's house count suggests that the frontage of each house was three times larger than that of houses in later times, and that that is unlikely. It is in-

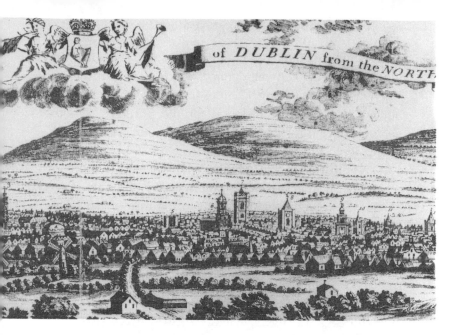

Prospect by Charles Brooking of Dublin from the north, 1728 (detail).

The old custom house and Essex Bridge at Dublin, 1753 (detail).

deed unlikely, since we know that house plots tended from the very outset to be well-defined, which made it difficult for developers to build larger houses in any ready way in subsequent years: try, for instance, for the purposes of some scheme of your own, buying your neighbour's house or garden. Moreover we know from the evidence of houses in Dublin and other cities that successive houses tended to occupy the same site and that rebuilding in existing built-up streets took up existing frontages. Even in the case of radical rebuilding, it was much easier to build a new house on the existing site than to attempt to enlarge the site to give a wider house frontage on the street. In any event, the preferred urban building option in Ireland and elsewhere tended to be a narrow two-bay house, providing on each floor two rooms, one front and rear, and a staircase. It was only on virgin sites and for new customers in quest of larger houses that the three- and, much less frequently, the four-bay house became common in central Dublin. Dublin was probably predominantly occupied by narrow houses. When building accelerated from the 1680s in the Liberties, many new houses, some on virgin sites, were narrow three-bay ones. Slightly larger than the old two-bay type, they reflected a new degree of ease and income.

Having started with a leap of imagination to conclude that there were at least 5,000 inhabitants in Dublin in about 1610, we could assume that houses were three times more numerous than Speed suggested. In other words the population perhaps did not exceed 15,000. If we believe that a household average of six is too small, we could assume that it was higher – say eight persons – as the city grew, and that the population was in excess of 15,000, say roughly 20,000 people. If we take a figure in the range of 15,000 to 20,000 as a crude approximation, then we have not only an estimate of the city's size, but a basis from which we may make comparisons with better figures for later years. We may conclude that the city either doubled or trebled in population between 1610 and 1680 to 40,000, then added another 20,000 by 1700, and trebled again in the eighteenth century.

With a population somewhere between 5,000 and 20,000, probably in the middle of that range, in 1610, it was a small city. But it was already a larger one than in the recent past. Dublin had not even been the invariable location of parliaments. Parliament as often as not met outside Dublin and in places as far away as Kilkenny or Drogheda. Foreign trade did not centre on Dublin either: Drogheda rivalled it for the cross-channel trade, and the trade with continental Europe was dominated by Galway and Waterford. We have a curious index of their importance in that it was the merchants or ship masters of these ports, and not of Dublin, who on their return were quizzed by officials for news of what was afoot in Europe.

What changed the fortunes of Dublin was the effort by English monarchs to conquer Ireland and to wear down the opposition, especially that in Ulster, which in many ways turned Ireland, especially for the last two decades of the sixteenth century, into England's Vietnam. Dublin became a military bridgehead for the conquest or reconquest of Ireland. Conquest meant armies and heavy official expenditure, and the sort of brittle prosperity that military adventures brought to Saigon in the 1960s in the effort to defeat the Vietcong. It also made the office of lord deputy important on a daily basis, and not merely on the occasions when a meeting of parliament approached. Hitherto the administration was overawed, sometimes even operated, by great Irish territorial magnates like the earls of Kildare. Now what impressed were the lord deputy, the castle and its ceremonial, as the sketches in John Derricke's *Image of Ireland* in 1581 suggested. With the war over in 1602, all could have faded away, but for the necessity to provide a new administration to look after a conquered kingdom. Parliaments henceforth met in Dublin alone, and the business of the courts, multiplying as plantation changed land title and made litigation endless, for the first time brought barristers and clients to the city from all parts of the country for protracted stays. If not good for the individuals caught up in it, litigation spelt prosperity for everyone else. We have a fleeting glimpse of Dublin life on the eve of all this change in the accounts of the clerk of works on Christ Church Cathedral that survive for 1565. The diet of the masons he employed was quite copious with wheaten bread, beef and fish, but a sharp contrast with the barley-brewed beverages of urban Europe resided in the generous allowance of 8 pints of ale a day, brewed principally from oaten malt. On Sundays the clerk of works sometimes took the masons out into the countryside for a day and entertained them.

In the wake of wartime prosperity and new – and regular – expenditures, Dublin began to grow. At first it still built houses in characteristic English half-timbered style, already the style of the central streets. The first measure of the physical growth of the city comes from Speed's map itself. On the north side of the river, beyond the city's sole bridge, a substantial quarter had grown up, and it was, it appears, into this district that livestock for the city came from the grazing grounds of Meath. On the south side the city had a line of houses running out west from Thomas Street, and another along The Coombe and into Cork Street. As the development of Thomas Street beyond the old corn market just outside the walls suggests, the provisioning of the city had outgrown the little market. To this street came the grain from Kildare that was essential for the city and, in the wide but crowded street, impatient buyers and sellers soon began to strike bargains before they got as far as the market-house. In later times it became the centre of the food and beverage industries, and especially of the whiskey distilleries and breweries, which consumed the barley that had been so little known in the city in 1600. The Coombe, the other line of houses, was in the valley of the river of the same name; it provided water, perhaps to drive a few mills, but mainly for the dyeing and finishing processes in the textile industry. It was here that the industry, the largest employer of labour in the city, was to develop.

Even eighty years after Speed had drawn his map, the development was incomplete. One of Francis Place's drawings in 1698, taken from the Liffey to the west of the city, showed that the walls near the river were intact and the ground open outside them. In essence the seventeenth-century expansion concentrated in two great bulges from the old walled city. The first bulge was in the district to the north, which filled out rapidly and made a second bridge necessary by 1670. A further and grander bridge, Essex Bridge in 1678, transferred northern expansion further east to the new line of Capel Street. Since this district, safely on the north bank of the Liffey, was well clear of the old city, and at first less crowded and also close to the amenity of the Phoenix Park, it was already a fashionable centre of residence and many of the gentry had their town houses there. Because parliament met infrequently – it did not sit at all from 1667 to 1692 – there was no reason for fashionable citizens to seek residence on the south side. The other bulge of urban development was a two-pronged one along the line of The Coombe/Cork Street and Thomas Street. As both lines of street became fully developed, off them and more especially in between them, in new courts and alleys, the textile workers became numerous.

In 1700, given the concentration of the city's spread on two outward bulges, it still preserved some of its past characteristics. St Stephen's Green, completed as an amenity in the 1660s, was slow to build up, and the space between it and the city was only incompletely developed. Grafton Street is a street of the 1720s. The city was of course changing. Two changes were visually most striking. First, new houses from as early as the 1620s were in brick; brick houses, too, began to replace existing wooden houses in the boom of the 1680s and onwards. Secondly, until the 1680s, the only important new public buildings were churches: the rebuilding of existing ones, the addition of spires and new houses of worship gave the city a skyline of towers and spires. Place's view of the city from the sea is one of a city of dreaming spires. In all, seventeen towers and spires can be counted. In Brooking's perspective of 1728, from a different angle as well as from a later date, at least twelve can be identified. Place's count, so striking at first glance, is not therefore exaggerated, even if the drama is probably heightened by the approach from the sea to a smaller city, compared with a view across countryside with a diminished perspective in a larger city thirty years later. Indeed, in Place's sketch, even from the sea the walls can be detected just as they can in his sketches from the west. In 1698 Dublin was still in a sense a walled city; in 1728 it was no longer one; the city had burst through them in all directions, and in all probability little more survived then than does today. Dublin in 1698 was already in the midst of a boom in its expansion. What Brooking's vignettes of 1728 mark, too, is the growth in civic buildings: parish churches had ceased to be the characteristic or dominant structures.

House building was intense in the Liberties from 1680 to 1720. It is often assumed that the textile industry was badly affected by the famous act of 1699 which prohibited the export of woollen goods. However, Dublin's industry catered only for the home market. By 1720 house building had exhausted the ground around the Liberties. The city's growth was now rapid in all directions: north of the Liffey, filling in the underdeveloped lands to the north-east; south of the river, moving to the east and south. On the north side it was commerce and residence; on the south side the chosen site of the new parliament house in 1728 (the Bank of Ireland to us) meant that the streets close to it and the green, so slow to develop, now expanded rapidly as an area of high amenity. Brooking's map of 1728 gives an impression of the city as it then was: in the pictorial perspective, taken from the north side, one can see that the houses already reached well into the countryside and, because the ground was rising, the artist had little difficulty in creating the impression of expansion in like fashion on the south side.

By 1800 Dublin was a very large city, the second largest in Britain or Ireland, and the sixth largest in western Europe. We have an unending stream of comment on it. The publication of Brooking's pictorial map in 1728 and the parliamentary decision to build a new parliament house are hardly coincidental. Between 1680 and 1728 the city had acquired many public buildings, and neat vignettes on the side of the map illustrate them: some are quite splendid. Moreover the location of the buildings shows how far the city had spread: the Royal Hospital of the 1680s was far to the west of the city on the south side, as was the Royal Barracks on the north bank, though not quite so far west as the Royal Hospital because the Phoenix Park as a royal park could not be encroached upon. The Linen Hall, already completed in 1728, was on rising ground on the north side. Downstream the buildings ran along the shores of the Liffey: one result was that Trinity College was no longer outside the city. A large and handsome custom house in 1708 was the first new public building within the old walled city, symbolically standing directly beside the prestigious Essex Bridge and its extension as Capel Street.

The city now continued to accumulate public buildings at a rapid rate. The great façade of Trinity College, raised in the 1750s and financed by the public purse, fronted the most massive single ensemble of collegiate architecture in Europe. The Royal Exchange followed in the 1770s. Public buildings so far, with the exception of the barracks and the Linen Hall, were on the south side of the river. But by the end of the century the erection of yet another and even grander custom house, and of the Four Courts and King's Inns on the north side of the river, emphasised that for a time at least political clout and public prestige had migrated to the north bank. Malton's prints celebrate the city in the 1790s, when the flow of improvements was in full spate. Indeed Malton himself had been employed by Gandon on the Custom House, which in turn was execrated by the radicals of the day, and was pronounced by Grattan in the commons to be of first-rate extravagance and sixth-rate architecture.

The Dublin of 1700 was essentially a Protestant city. However, as its growth accelerated in the eighteenth century, it drew in population in large numbers from the surrounding counties. Fate had decreed that, in contrast to counties further afield, the neighbouring counties, apart from Wicklow, had very small Protestant populations. The consequences were that in all probability, as the population soared in mid-century, two or even three out of every four immigrants from the rural hinterland were Catholic. Just as striking as the pace of the city's growth is that, whereas the early growth of the city had been northwards and westwards, it was from the 1740s predominantly eastwards. As a result much of the city's development spilt out on to ground that was a floodplain in the seventeenth century and the foundations of the new buildings in the eighteenth century were awash in the rise and fall of the tidal water-table. The old city itself had chosen higher ground, just as the fashionable developments in the early decades of the eighteenth century in Henrietta Street or around St Stephen's Green chose high ground. With the exception of St Stephen's Green, which was safely south of the prevailing air flow across the old city and its industrial districts, the new districts were to the windward of the city: the prevailing wind wafted in their direction the noisome smoke of tanneries, brickworks and process industries and of the growing number of domestic chimneys. Even until a few years ago, if the wind was from the west, the sweet odour of brewing from Guinness's could be scented on O'Connell Bridge or in College Park. The problems were well known to contemporaries: some parliamentary measures in the eighteenth century were directed towards driving various industries westwards. The green never became unfashionable, even at the height of the Gardiner development in the 1750s, 1760s and 1770s on the north side.

Precluded from spreading westwards on the north side by the presence of the park and barracks, and on the south side by the dense housing of the Liberties, by the amenity district of the Royal Hospital, and around it by the noisome industries driven from the centre, the eastward drive of the city was inevitable. This meant, too, that some of the new districts, though visualised as residential, were under enormous pressure from the start: with relief roads to the east precluded by the presence of the sea, the bridges and the associated eastward move of the port and custom house ensured that the central residential streets would eventually become corridors of through communication. The controversy from the 1740s to the late 1770s over the building of a new bridge and over the siting of a new custom house underlines the critical problem of north-south communication in a residential city that could not spread westwards. In building a new residential quarter in and eastwards of Sackville Street (now O'Connell Street) and in erecting a new river crossing further downstream, the Beresford/Gardiner faction who promoted the concept and whose political clout alone made it possible seem to have failed to advert to the conflict of interest between the creation of residential districts and at the same time the generation of novel pressures on residential amenity.

Dublin's development is often regarded as planned. There are two elements in Dublin planning. The first is the central guidance of the ground landlord, which we have to admit was not particularly successful before the 1780s. The second element, something of a political stroke engineered by politicians, is concerned primarily with streetscapes. The city by the 1790s had spread out to the line of the new circular roads, or rather on the south side to the line of the new canal, where the Grand Canal was planned as an amenity. It was envisaged in the 1790s that the city would expand in the same fashion on the north side, and until the 1820s the outline of new streets and of a grand crescent, projected in the 1790s, continued to be etched in on maps. However, the north side had already begun to lose its residential appeal. From the north the shore line, which became Amiens Street after 1802, brought traffic inwards, and the opening of the route from Mountjoy Square to the custom house – Gardiner Street – became a relief road to both Amiens Street and Sackville Street. From the west the Broadstone with its canal docks (and later railway station) channelled traffic directly into what had been one of the city's grandest streets, Dominick Street, and even Rutland Square. On the south side the bulk of business came from Kildare and beyond; even the traffic from Wexford and east Wicklow moved well inland once it passed through Bray in order to reach Thomas Street. Hence the Fitzwilliam estate (or the Pembroke estate as it became) was largely untouched. The railway from Westland Row, though the first to be built, was the slowest to be extended, and the least busy with commerce. Fashionable Dublin moved from the Gardiner estate to the Fitzwilliam estate, and less than a generation later from that to its outer reaches, already known as the Pembroke estate. The railway station funnelled traffic directly into the city centre towards the river crossings, not into the Pembroke estate itself, and ironically alone of the railways the Westland Row line was successful as a suburban railway, servicing an almost uninterrupted and largely unspoiled amenity district from Merrion Square out to Dún Laoghaire and ultimately to Bray and Greystones.

The spread along the coast altered the city. From one point of view, it drew the city's comfortable classes outwards. It was now Monkstown rather than Mountjoy Square, just as Mountjoy Square and the other squares had a half-century to a century previously attracted prosperous citizens from the old and once crowded centre. The historic centre itself was by the late nineteenth century occupied by commerce, slums and worship. It is an irony, too, that with further change today the slums and commerce alike have left the medieval core of the city. Many of the old parish churches still stand, either in use or now without congregations. The cathedrals remain as well, and their towers remain the dominant feature of the skyline. But while they continue to attract lively congregations, many of the worshippers themselves speed in by bus or by car from the suburbs.

Select bibliography
P. Butel and L. M. Cullen (eds): *Cities and Merchants: French and Irish Perspectives on Urban Development 1500–1900*, Dublin, 1986.
M. Craig: *Dublin 1660–1860*, Dublin, 1949.
L. M. Cullen: *Townlife*, Dublin, 1973.
L. M. Cullen: *Princes and Pirates: the Dublin Chamber of Commerce 1783–1983*, Dublin, 1983.
L. M. Cullen: 'The growth of Dublin 1600–1900: character and heritage', in F. H. A. Aalen and K. Whelan (eds), *Dublin City and County: from Prehistory to Present*, Dublin, 1992, pp. 251–78.

M. E. Daly: *Dublin, the Deposed Capital: a Social and Economic History 1860–1914*, Cork, 1985.

J. Harvey: *Dublin: a Study in Environment*, London, 1949.

C. Lennon: *The Lords of Dublin in the Age of Reformation*, Dublin, 1989.

J. H. Martin: 'The social geography of mid-nineteenth-century Dublin city', in W. J. Smyth and K. Whelan (eds), *Common Ground: Essays on the Historical Geography of Ireland*, Cork, 1988, pp. 173–88.

J. Warburton, J. Whitelaw and R. Walsh: *History of the City of Dublin*, London, 1818.

FROM CITY SLUMS TO CITY SPRAWL: DUBLIN FROM 1800 TO THE PRESENT

Jacinta Prunty

IN the early nineteenth century it was easy to identify where Dublin city officially ended and the suburbs began: the municipal boundary, following mostly the line of the Royal Canal to the north and the Grand Canal to the south, provided a clear-cut administrative area, which still included acres of open space. To encircle Dublin today would be a very different experience. So massively extended is the city that early landmarks are difficult to identify. The separate identity of surrounding villages such as Clondalkin, Crumlin, Donnybrook, Finglas, Killester, Raheny, Rathfarnham and Tallaght has been obliterated. The city has literally been turned inside out, in terms of both population and physical structure: the 1991 population of 1,024,429 for the greater Dublin district dwarfs the 1841 city population of under 233,000; more than 92 per cent of Dubliners now live outside the canals, with development extending to the north, south and west, and even to the north-east as far as reclamation from the sea has allowed. Vast low-density municipal and private housing estates extend ever further into the agricultural hinterland. Geographers no longer speak of Dublin as a 'city' but as a 'city-region', as its commuting zone spreads beyond county boundaries into Kildare, Meath and Wicklow.

As the nineteenth century opens we find Dublin city in the

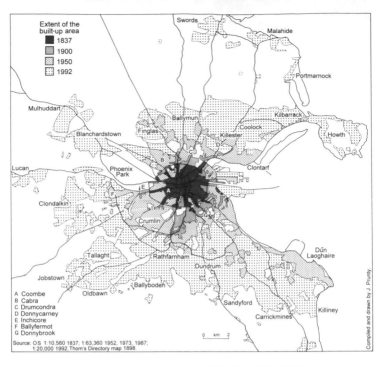

Compiled and drawn by J. Prunty

Extent of the
built-up area
■ 1837
▨ 1900
▦ 1950
▒ 1992

A Coombe
B Cabra
C Drumcondra
D Donnycarney
E Inchicore
F Ballyfermot
G Donnybrook

Source: OS 1:10,560 1837; 1:63,360 1952, 1973, 1987;
1:20,000 1992, Thom's Directory map 1898.

0   km   2

Map showing the growth of Dublin, 1837–1992.

grip of a cholera epidemic, its virulence increased by crop failure. In an effort to bring the epidemic under control a group of
physicians promoted the establishment of a specialised fever
hospital or, as it was more hopefully titled, the House of Recovery in Cork Street on what was then the south-western
fringe of the built-up area. They campaigned on two fronts:
firstly to establish a purpose-built hospital, detached from all
other buildings, in an airy situation, to which fever patients
could rapidly be removed; and secondly to counteract the progress of infection by tackling what they regarded as its source
– the immense heaps of putrid matter piled up in close and
confined back yards. But before the citizens could be gal-
vanised into action, they had to be convinced that infectious
diseases such as cholera, typhus and smallpox which periodically swept through the city did not appear in some inexplica-

ble fashion, but were directly related to the close and dirty living conditions of the slums.

Once generated, disease spread uncontrollably from room to room and from floor to floor through well-meaning visits from fellow residents. Distant houses of the rich were also vulnerable, as disease was carried back from the tenements through the visits of servants to friends and relations. Dealing in foodstuffs and especially in second-hand clothes also hastened the spread of sickness. In Dublin there was as yet little geographical distance between the rich and the poor, so that the question of epidemic disease could not be ignored. Nowhere, and no one, was safe.

Among a succession of courageous individuals who risked infection to survey the homes of Dublin's poor, the Reverend James Whitelaw provided the most incisive study. The problems that he identified in his report of 1805 were to form the substance of innumerable reports for more than a century: overcrowding; the tenement system of subdivision of houses, and even of individual rooms, to meet exorbitant rents; the disgraceful state of the sanitary accommodation, described by Whitelaw 'in painful and often disgusting detail'. Human waste was only one part of the problem: private dung-yards, dairy-yards, and slaughter-houses, overcrowded cemeteries, and obnoxious activities such as soap-making and lime-burning right in the midst of this crowded population – all added to the problems. Underpinning all was the appalling poverty of so many of the citizens.

Outbreaks of cholera in 1818 and again in 1832 were accompanied by further heart-breaking accounts of the living conditions in the poorer districts both north and south of the Liffey. Typical was the scene in Hamilton's Court off Skinner's Alley in The Coombe where three narrow houses sheltered 182 inmates, described as 'principally mendicant lodgers, in abject misery and want' who were formerly 'industriously employed in the woollen, cotton and silk line'; the houses faced on to an open sewer that was choked up with stagnant and putrefactive matter. Such scandalous scenes continued for decades, as the evidence of charity visitors and witnesses to official inquiries testify. Margaret Aylward, who organised a relief network in the north city in the 1850s, described her visits up crumbling staircases and out to stable dwellings with earthen floors, where the rain and wind had free entry, and the sick person lay waiting for death on a heap of worn straw. And all too often such a wretched bed was shared with several relations. Malnutrition left people especially vulnerable to sickness. Dr Speer, who was attached to the city dispensary, reported in 1822 that potatoes were practically the sole item on the menu for most Dubliners, accompanied by tea, which he condemned as nutritionally worthless, but from which he could never wean them. At the turn of the century lady sanitary officers regularly came across pregnant women who, in the struggle to provide for their existing children, could not themselves afford to eat for several days together.

It was a constant source of amazement to inspectors and commentators that such wretchedness could be found even in the most respectable districts, such as off Mount Street and Clare Street. In fact no part of the city was without its hidden sores. In Lacy's Lane, near Merrion Square, the situation of the residents, mostly female, was described as 'nothing but one scene of filth, misery and want' although 'in the vicinity of one of our best squares, within the wealthiest parish in the metropolis [sic]'.

Despite such public knowledge the Dublin slum situation was allowed to continue unchecked until the middle of the nineteenth century. Up to 1848 the city's sanitary matters were nominally the charge of the individual parishes, and the gross inadequacy of this system needs no comment. To render the city a healthy place for all required the continuous efforts of a

Decayed Georgian houses at the rear of North Cumberland Street, Dublin, 1913.

single municipal authority that had both extensive powers relating to public health, and the funds to implement the necessary reforms. The turning point came at mid-century, with the transfer of powers from the old Paving Board and the Wide Streets Commissioners to the reformed Dublin Corporation, marking the beginning of administrative efficiency and the consolidation of authority in relation to public health. Co-inciding with municipal reform was the beginning of effective legislation, with the Nuisances Removal and Diseases Prevention Act, and the Public Health Act, both passed in 1848. While it was not until more workable legislation was enacted in the 1870s that the battle to rid the city of 'fever nests' was undertaken in earnest, the mid-century reforms set the stage for progress.

But where to start in a situation where there were so many urgent needs? The regulation of common lodging-houses, the licensing of slaughter-houses and the issuing of innumerable orders to 'abate nuisances' first occupied the time of the small sanitary staff, backed up by two 'inspectors of nuisances' drawn from the Dublin Metropolitan Police. The appointment of the city's first medical officer of health, Dr Mapother, in 1864 marked the beginning of a serious approach to public health, while his successor Dr Cameron was a tireless and effective campaigner. The corporation's shining success was the adoption of the Vartry water scheme in 1863–8, providing the citizens with a reliable supply of the purest water, the envy of many other cities at the time. The sewerage problem was to take longer to resolve. There were 109 miles of streets in the city in 1850, but only 39 miles of sewers, so that the corporation inherited a mammoth engineering task no less urgent than that of the water supply. The Main Drainage Scheme was eventually started in 1892 (completed 1906), while the formidable task of connecting up individual houses to the main sewers was ongoing.

The real centre of attention shifted to the housing situation. It had taken considerable time and pressure to move the local authority to provide services that were plainly best provided on a collective basis, such as street scavenging and proper sewers. To follow logically through to the forcible closure of filthy decrepit tenements, wholesale clearance and the rehousing of those displaced were to take many decades. The passing of permissive and cumbersome legislation, such as the Cross Act in 1875, did little to aid slum clearance when the will to implement it was absent.

In an initial burst of optimism in 1879, the corporation undertook the clearance of a block of 110 houses in The Coombe and handed over the site at a nominal sum to the newly-formed Dublin Artisans' Dwellings Company for house-building. But the experience proved so complex and expensive, and in any case was of no assistance to those displaced, that the corporation resolved to focus on the inspection and closure of the most appalling of the tenement houses instead. It was a painfully slow, legalistic process that met with limited success. There was little movement on other fronts. Very few Dublin businesses provided housing for workers. Watkins Brewery was among the exceptions, while the Iveagh Trust, a philanthropic company founded by the Guinness dynasty, was to make a substantial contribution to the housing and care of the poor in its block dwellings in Patrick Street and Kevin Street. However, the vast majority of the city's population continued to pay extortionist rents for substandard private accommodation.

In the later nineteenth century public debate crystallised around the single-room tenement system as being at the heart of Dublin's problems. In their flight to the suburbs the wealthy vacated substantial town-houses in once-aristocratic districts such as Gardiner Street and Summer Hill on the north side. These one-family homes were rapidly subdivided to accommodate at best one family per room, but with little structural change. One observer summed up the situation:

> Within this space the food of these wretched beings, such as it is, must be prepared; within this space they must eat and drink; men, women and children must strip, dress, sleep. In cases of illness the calls of nature must be relieved; and when death releases one of the inmates, the corpse must of necessity remain for days within the room.

Usually four storeys in height, there was no direct means of removing the refuse from each floor, so that the common stairs soon became fouled, and the provision of piped water and bathrooms to each unit was impractical. A toilet in an outside yard shared by fifteen or sixteen families was difficult to keep clean, particularly when anyone could come in off the street and use it. In the complex web of Dublin property holding, with perhaps five owners to one tenement house along with immediate lessees, tenants, subtenants and occupiers, it was often impossible to determine who was responsible for repairs. Enforcing health regulations often led to more distress, as the former tenants, unable to pay higher rents for the improved dwellings, overcrowded other tenements. In a city in which there was so little remunerative employment 'house jobbing', or the subletting of property, was an important source of income among the poor as well as among the better-off. And these circumstances were not at all confined to a small if distressed section of the population; over one-third of the citizens lived in such unacceptable conditions in 1894.

The outmigration of the wealthy to exclusive self-governing suburban townships, such as Pembroke, Rathmines and later Clontarf, gathered pace in the later nineteenth century. From here the better-off were spared the smells and dirt of the old city, the sight of its beggars and homeless, the dangers of contagion, but could still travel in by tram or train to avail themselves fully of all that the city offered in terms of com-

116

merce and culture. They could offload their servants to the city hospitals and workhouses without having to contribute to their upkeep in the form of rates or hospital charges; such costs were all carried by those still foolish enough to be living inside the city boundary. While of course the township residents had local charges to pay, they were lower than the city rates and these residents enjoyed much tighter control over exactly how their contributions were spent. The city's financial basis was being eroded just as the range and standard of services it was expected to provide increased phenomenally. The struggle to expand the city boundaries to include all the townships was not won until 1930.

As the nineteenth century closed, one important yardstick was used to measure the condition of the Dublin poor against that of urban dwellers elsewhere – the rate of mortality. In 1899 the death rate reached the outrageous figure of 33.6 per 1,000 persons for the Dublin city area; the London average was 19.6. The high Dublin rate was due largely to the prevalence of pulmonary tuberculosis, also known as consumption or the 'wasting disease', most of whose victims were aged around 25 years. The major obstacle to its eradication was persuading the citizenry that TB was contagious rather than hereditary, very difficult to accept as one family member after another succumbed. Free disinfection, for example, was offered to the residents of any Dublin dwelling in which a person suffering from consumption had died, but in three cases out of four the offer was refused. One doctor proclaimed in frustration that 'they will attend wakes, sleep, dwell or visit, in places teeming with infection, without a moment's misgiving, but as soon as ever the officer has been brought to disinfect a house or room, they shun it as if he had brought the plague instead of banishing it'.

The TB crusade in the first decade of this century became inextricably linked with the slum housing question, while

117

public opinion in favour of direct State intervention was growing. However, the expense of earlier ventures in the city centre directed attention outwards, beyond the two canals. The 'suburban solution' was proposed in 1903, as part of the 'garden city' and town planning movements then gaining international credibility. But before there was a clear-cut move in this direction, the inadequacy of Dublin Corporation's response to the slum problem resulted in a comprehensive investigation being imposed by the Local Government Board in 1913. Photographs of tiny cabins packed into the back yards of once-fashionable houses, and tenement rooms equipped with little more than a verminous straw mattress and tin cup, were used to illustrate the written report and statistical tables. As the inquiry got under way the reasons for the poverty that created this accommodation scandal were painfully clear: the deep-seated injustices in the Dublin labour market exploded in the Dublin Lock-out of 1913.

The outbreak of the First World War and escalating building costs led to the shelving of housing plans, while the Rising of 1916 and the struggle for independence focused energies in new directions. One government official claimed that the loss of life, the vast material waste, and what he termed 'the rebirth of dying antagonisms' of the Easter Rising might possibly have been avoided if the people of Dublin had been better housed. In the aftermath of the Rising the Westminster administration made a rapid effort to regain some of the lost momentum. In July 1917 P. C. Cowan, chief engineering inspector, was appointed to take the housing needs of Dublin as detailed in the damning 1914 Local Government report, and to produce a complete scheme to eliminate in time all insanitary dwellings. The task ahead was frighteningly simple: to plan an overall scheme of improved housing for almost 30,000 families, at least 41 per cent of the city's population. The method was to be two-fold: 16,500 new, self-contained houses to meet over half of the required number of family units, the remainder to be created in remodelled tenement houses. Sites for most of the new houses were available in Cabra, Clontarf, Crumlin and Drumcondra – all possibilities since the first extension of the city boundary in 1900 to include the north city and Inchicore townships.

As the gradual but inexorable move towards mass suburbanisation took hold, there was a sharp condemnation of previous piecemeal efforts. The thrust was towards tackling the slum crisis in the context of an integrated and visionary master plan for the 'Dublin of the future'. The Civics Institute launched a major international competition to produce such a plan in 1914; the winning entry, that of Patrick Abercrombie and partners of Liverpool University, was not published until 1922. In that year the restoration of capital city status to Dublin brought huge changes in the political and economic agenda. Most noticeable is the surge of pride and hope in Dublin, described as 'a city of magnificent possibilities, not even inferior to Paris', and requiring only wise planning to realise these.

The Civic Survey of 1925 provided an inventory of the city's assets in terms such as manufacturing, transport infrastructure, medical services, and recreation facilities. The hygiene and housing maps make a graphic introduction to the task facing the new State: most of the city centre is one vast expanse of black and grey, depicting insanitary areas, tenement dwellings, decayed and dangerous buildings, with isolated pockets of new housing, such as in Bull Alley and John Dillon Street, appearing as very small oases in a desert of decay.

Against this dismal geography of the early twentieth century, no hope at all was held out for remaking the city centre as a place in which to live. Some large city-centre flat complexes such as Oliver Bond and Bridgefoot Street were built in the 1930s, but overall hopes for the future were pinned on the suburban dream. The reluctance of many city residents to move out to the unknown wilds of Cabra and Crumlin was brushed aside as 'a traditional, but regrettable, attachment to congested surroundings', from which the delights of suburban life would soon wean them.

The strength of the suburban argument rested on the provision of cheap and efficient public transport: electric tram or motor bus would link suburb and city in 10 or 12 minutes, allowing the labourer to commute to work. It was also expected that industry would relocate to take advantage of the cheaper suburban sites and the ready source of labour. Rather than being denied work, it was argued that such a move would double male earning opportunities; female work opportunities were discounted. The garden suburbs themselves were to contain all that was considered necessary to a healthy and wholesome life: shops, schools, churches, neighbourhood centres, allotments for cultivating vegetables, children's playgrounds, and facilities for such civilised recreation as bowling.

While there was little need for any further research on the Dublin slum problem, there was great urgency to improve the planning system so that development could proceed in an orderly way. In 1936 the city council adopted a resolution to prepare a planning scheme for the whole municipal area under section 29 of the Town and Regional Planning Act, 1934; in 1941, in the middle of the war, Abercrombie presented his second Dublin plan. While his main concern had shifted to making the city a monumental place, the focus of national pride and administration, he recognised the danger of unrestricted urban sprawl. To prevent Dublin city from expanding to what he called 'monstrous dimensions', he proposed the imposition of a 'green belt' varying between four and six miles wide circling the built-up area. Further population increase, he suggested, should be accommodated in a group of satellite towns, similarly separated from the city and from each other by green belts. In this sketch development plan Abercrombie moved the agenda forward from considering the city in isolation to planning its future as part of a larger region.

Following immediately on the end of the Second World War, however, an impressive catalogue of suburban developments was undertaken by the corporation. The opening-up of Ballyfermot, Cabra West and Donnycarney in the 1940s marked the first large-scale population movements out of the inner city; in the 1950s Coolock and Finglas were important destinations; in the 1960s Ballymun came to the fore. But it was the Advisory Regional Plan for the Dublin metropolitan area produced by Myles Wright in 1967 that opened up the western suburbs to the burgeoning city population. The decision to concentrate future development in four western new towns – Blanchardstown, Clondalkin/Lucan, and Tallaght – echoes part of Abercrombie's 1941 plan for satellite towns, but the population numbers that these new towns would accommodate were beyond what he or anyone else could have foreseen. The four new towns, based on existing villages but growing westwards in a linear fashion and separated from each other by green wedges, were intended to hold between 60,000 to 100,000 persons each. While the new towns stretched the city westwards, development continued along its southern and northern fringes, too, as widespread car ownership brought ever more distant areas within daily reach, changing the shape of the city-region for good.

The closing paragraph of the 1925 Civic Survey provides a fitting note on which to end. The survey presented a comprehensive and sobering account of the immense problems facing the capital city of the new State, not least of which was its tenement cancer. In reflective mood the author describes Dublin as 'a city redolent of charm; a city of castle, sea and distant hills; a city full-charged with the glory and pathos of the past'. He concludes with the rousing challenge, 'Let her citizens resolve that Dublin shall have a great future'.

Select bibliography

F. H. A. Aalen: 'Health and housing in Dublin: past, present and future', in F. H. A. Aalen and K. Whelan (eds), *Dublin City and County: from Prehistory to Present*, Dublin, 1992, pp. 279–304.

J. Brady: 'Dublin: change and challenge', in H. Clout (ed.), *Europe's Cities in the Late Twentieth Century*, Amsterdam, 1994, pp. 69–84.

L. M. Cullen: 'The growth of Dublin 1600–1900: character and heritage', in F. H. A. Aalen and K. Whelan (eds), *Dublin City and County: from Prehistory to Present*, Dublin, 1992, pp. 252–7.

M. E. Daly: *Dublin, the Deposed Capital: a Social and Economic History, 1860–1914*, Cork, 1985.

A. Horner: 'From city to city region: Dublin from the 1930s to the 1990s', in F. H. A. Aalen and K. Whelan (eds), *Dublin City and County: from Prehistory to Present*, Dublin, 1992, pp. 327–58.

A. Horner and A. J. Parker (eds): *Geographical Perspectives on the Dublin Region*, Dublin, 1987.

K. C. Kearns: *Dublin Tenement Life, an Oral History*, Dublin, 1994.

A. MacLaran: *Dublin, the Shaping of a Capital*, London, 1993.

J. H. Martin: 'The social geography of mid-nineteenth-century Dublin city', in W. J. Smith and K. Whelan (eds), *Common Ground: Essays on the Historical Geography of Ireland*, Cork, 1988, pp. 173–88.

B. Murnane: 'The recreation of the urban historical landscape: Mountjoy Ward, Dublin c. 1901', in W. J. Smith and K. Whelan (eds), *Common Ground: Essays on the Historical Geography of Ireland*, Cork, 1988, pp. 189–207.

J. Prunty: *Dublin Slums 1800–1925: a Study in Urban Geography*, Dublin, 1995.

MEDIEVAL GALWAY: DEPENDENCE AND LIBERTY

Gearóid Mac Niocaill

THE core of Galway first appears in 1124, when the castle of Bun Gaillimhe, 'the mouth of the [River] Gaillimh' (now the Corrib), was built for Toirrdelbach Ua Conchobair, king of Connacht, in the earlier stages of his rise to dominance. It was a good choice of site, since it controlled the most convenient crossing from east to west, on a river easily forded and indeed liable at times to dry up almost completely, as in 1462, when 'many things were found', according to the annals. The castle was probably some kind of timber structure or stockade, fairly easily destroyed, as it was in 1132, and as quickly rebuilt; and it appears to have had some kind of settlement around it already in 1149, when it was destroyed again – a recurrent risk, since it was burnt in 1161 and again in 1170. In the Anglo-Norman invasion of Connacht it was captured in 1230 by Richard de Burgo, recovered in 1233 by Feidlim Ua Conchobair, and almost immediately taken again by De Burgo; thereafter, despite occasional destruction by fire, as in 1247, it was firmly under the control of the De Burgos.

While these probably thought of Galway primarily as a military strong-point, they also realised that the revenue from the settlement that had grown around the castle was worth protecting, and the next logical step was to obtain, in about 1270, a grant of murage for Galway, i.e., the right to levy toll on certain specified goods such as hides and fleeces, fish and

Pictorial map by Barnaby Gooche of Galway in 1583.

wine, salt and cloth, coming into the town, to finance the building of town walls. Only small sums were involved, but over a
period of almost ten years the collectors made a little over £57
and managed to get the walls built for a little over £46. These
walls, enclosing an area of about 25 acres, were added to in
1312, when the great gate was erected. The sums gathered for
building the walls are at the same time an indication of the
growing importance of the town as a source of profit. We do
not know what the population was, but there was obviously a
sufficiently numerous and well-off body of inhabitants to finance the building of the church of St Nicholas of Myra, patron
of seafarers, about 1320. The legal structures of the town at this
period were probably not much different from those of other
seignorial towns such as Kilkenny and New Ross, in which
rents were fixed and the lord's prerogatives willingly limited,
to attract settlers. Nevertheless, it was still the lord's town, and

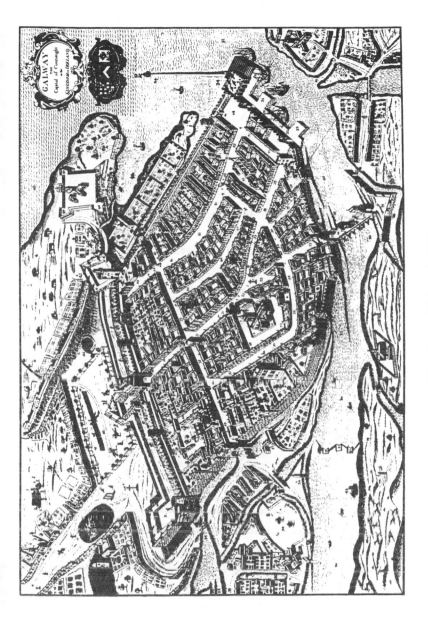

Pictorial map of Galway in 1651.

125

the town court was the lord's court, bringing in to the Red Earl a handy £5 yearly by 1326, and a further profit in lands escheated to him for lack of heirs or for felony. Down to the murder of William de Burgo, the Brown Earl, in 1333, the town was probably held on a fairly tight rein.

The Brown Earl's heir was his infant daughter, Elizabeth; but his Connacht lands were seized by her cousins, and for some years there was a rather confused struggle for supremacy between Edmund, a younger son of the Red Earl, and the sons of William Liath de Burgo, the Red Earl's first cousin, which was settled in 1338 when one of these latter, Eamonn Albanach, captured Edmund, tied a stone round his neck, and dropped him into Lough Mask. By 1340 Eamonn Albanach was firmly established in the Burke lands in north Connacht, and his brother William took over the lands in County Galway. This made him, in addition, *de facto* lord of the town of Galway, and his own heavy involvement and that of his sons in the wars of Connacht was liable to draw Galway in also, and to its detriment. The precise degree of control, of course, varied with the current level of dissension among the Burkes themselves, and with the extent to which the Dublin government was able to exercise authority and influence in the area, as exemplified by such things as appointments of customs officials. But all in-all, the Burkes in the fourteenth century were of necessity uncomfortable neighbours and lords. It is probable that the leading families of the town tried to play off the government against the Burkes. There was still contact with Dublin, since the provost and bailiffs of Galway got a grant of murage in 1361 for five years and the grant was renewed in 1366. Nevertheless, by 1388 it is clear that William Burke was in practice master of the town, and that the burgesses, willy-nilly, would support him against the king's officials. Probably they had no great choice in the matter: in 1390, when the bishop of Clonmacnoise was sent to Galway to investigate disorders there, he was refused an escort by the sheriff of Connacht. The submissions gained by Richard II on his first expedition to Ireland included that of William Burke of Clanricard, and the burgesses seized the opportunity of this general atmosphere of submissiveness, in 1396, to get for themselves what privileges and immunities they could, for a down payment of £6 13s. 4d. They got the right to elect yearly a sovereign and reeves, which they were already doing, and the franchises granted to Drogheda.

Precisely what did Galway gain by being given the franchises of Drogheda, the two parts of which, on the side of Meath and on the side of Louth, were to be amalgamated into a single unit sixteen years later? Basically it gave the burgesses a legal right to keep outsiders from any position of power or responsibility within the town. Only burgesses might trade within the town, and their elected officers had the right, and duty, to check the weights and measures used in trade. No outsider might serve on a jury within the town, and while a burgess continued to reside in the town he could not be summoned to serve on a jury outside the town nor indeed be appointed as a royal official outside the town – a useful privilege, since most royal officials at this period in Ireland ended up in trouble or in debt, or both. Similarly, a burgess could not be taken to law outside the town over land in the town. Even royal officials could not lodge either themselves or their retinues in the town without the burgesses' permission. Effectively, then, practically all jurisdiction within the town was placed securely in the citizens' hands, up to and including felonies, to be dealt with in their fortnightly court; and they had the further advantage of being able to use the archaic procedure of oath-helpers, which survived much longer in boroughs than elsewhere: a burgess accused of felony could go free if he could find forty others willing to swear that they believed in his innocence. No man or institution in the fourteenth century, it is fair to say, exercised justice for its own sake: they did so for the sake of profit. However, while their independent jurisdiction was cherished for the protection it offered against outsiders, the profits of the town court were liable to be slight, by virtue of the limitations placed on the level of fines that could be imposed on townsmen – usually, following the example of Drogheda, set at 12d. To add to the town's income, other privileges were called into play – odds and ends, such as the right to the property of convicted felons or of jail-breakers, and more regular ones, such as taxes on goods brought for sale to the weekly market and the annual fair: small amounts, measured in farthings, halfpennies and pennies, which could yet, on the principle of 'many a mickle makes a muckle', add up with luck to a respectable sum. All in all, then, a very respectable measure of autonomy; yet one clause in the grant could vitiate all the rest – the clause that reserved to the lord of the aforesaid town of Galway and his heirs, the rents, services, fines, issues and other profits pertaining to them, as lords of the said town, from the said town and its courts as they have hitherto had them freely and quietly or have been accustomed and entitled and in the habit to levy them by law.

Who, then, was the lord of the town? In theory, it was Roger Mortimer, fourth earl of March and seventh earl of Ulster, whom Richard II left behind as one of his two lieutenants in Ireland; in practice, it was still William Burke, Uilleag an Fhiona, who had been knighted by Richard at his departure. It would be up to the burgesses to make what they could of their privileges. At the same time there was another interesting development, in the burgesses' dealings with the Church. Some time in the last years of Pope Urban VI, before 1389, the men of Galway submitted a petition on the status of St Nicholas's. From time out of mind it had been held by the Cistercian abbey of Knockmoy, some 18 miles away in east Galway, which collected the revenues – tithes and offerings – and appointed a vicar, sometimes a secular priest, sometimes a religious, and removed him as the fancy took the abbot. The mills of the Roman curia ground slowly, then as now, and it was not until 1398 that the burgesses had an answer to their satisfaction, with the establishment of a permanent vicarage with revenues assigned to it. Knockmoy still took two-thirds of the revenues, but the remainder, the tithes of fish and the offerings or altarages, worth about £6–£7 a year, were assigned to the vicar.

This seems an appropriate point to stand back and look less at institutions and events – such as the fires of 1412 and 1473 – than at the people of the town. That there were burgesses of considerable wealth in Galway is obvious from the documents of the Blake family from the time of the earliest Blake onwards: this was Richard Cadell, nicknamed Niger or Black, who is found accumulating lands in County Galway (as it is now) as early as 1278; he was provost of Galway in 1290 and again in 1312, and sheriff of Connacht from 1303 to 1306. Generation after generation, the Blakes traded in hides and wine and salt, bought, leased and mortgaged lands inside and outside Galway and Athenry, and engaged in periodic bouts of litigation with one another over the division of lands. In their wills are to be found accounts of their movable property and their holdings: Henry Blake's will in 1451, and Wadin Blake's in 1499, list to the point of tedium houses and lands and dues in Galway and all over east Galway, for their children to fight over. Wealth, in this period, could of course be assessed in more than one way: by the amount of land a man owned, by the range and quality of his movable goods, perhaps by his credit (the amount he owed), and rather more riskily by the amount owed to him. A man such as Wadin Blake, as portrayed in his will in 1499, leaving numerous pieces of land of unspecified area, a quarry, various rents, and household goods such as brass pots, skillets, a large chest and a number of silver cups, along with trading commodities such as linen, wine and honey, most of which are left unvalued, and a small amount of cash, together with the money owed him, would rank more or less with the leading men of an Italian town such as Pisa.

Perhaps a more satisfactory way of estimating the burgesses' wealth is by looking at what they were able to give away; for example, by their patronage of the Dominican priory of Athenry, which seems to have been a particular object of charity for the burgesses of both towns, especially after the disastrous fire of about 1420. Take Edmund Lynch, who died in 1462 and was buried in the tomb that he had built in the Lady Chapel of St Nicholas's Church in Galway: he was a lavish patron of the Dominicans, both in buildings and in ornaments and vestments. The sixteen marks he paid for one set of vestments would, by contemporary reckoning, have kept one man adequately, though not luxuriously, for eight years. All this generosity was, of course, made possible by rents from lands and by the profits of trade; but our knowledge of the trade of Galway in the thirteenth, fourteenth and fifteenth centuries is far from satisfactory. We have stray glimpses of the trade in those ships that got into trouble – the ship *Magdeleyne* from Drogheda making for Bordeaux by a roundabout route, which was driven by bad weather into Galway in 1340, and there the captain was gulled out of his cargo by three unscrupulous locals named Richard Lok, Philip Mason and William le Long; or another glimpse, in 1416, of a Portuguese ship trading between Galway and Flanders and Normandy. Much of this trade was done by a kind of coasting: there is one case of a ship in trouble with the customs in Southampton in 1340–41, with a cargo put together in Carrickfergus, Galway and Waterford; and the converse of that is the ship *Julian* that did well in 1453, selling eighty-six tuns of wine in Galway, Burrishoole and Sligo. But it is impossible to piece together a systematic picture of the medieval trade of Galway from such evidence.

Some things we can, however, say with certainty. One is

that the basis of Galway's export trade was such items as hides. From 1275 onwards a custom was levied on exports of wool and hides at the rate of 6s. 8d. on every sack of wool or 300 fleeces, and 13s. 4d. on every 200 hides. We have figures for Galway for most of the last quarter of the thirteenth century and for the sixteen or so years in question exports averaged 6,600 hides a year – I say hides, because all the evidence points to these rather than to wool. After that the custom of Galway was farmed out for a flat £20 a year, the equivalent of 6,000 hides, and when Walter Blake was appointed keeper of the custom in 1346 it was still worth only £22. Modest though it was, it seems to have been steady, and up to 6,000 cattle perished year after year in the hinterland of Galway, east, west, north and south, though there is the stray reference to cargoes of wool: Geoffrey Blake got into trouble in 1395 for exporting wool without clearing it at the staple. There had been a staple in Galway, established for three years in 1375, but it was ended in 1377; and by the early fifteenth century there was not even a regular customs official in Galway. In 1415 a group of Galway merchants were among those loading hides on a Hanseatic ship from Lübeck in Galway, which was unable to put in to Kinsale to pay the custom, on account of bad weather. It was a trade, too, that established links between the merchants of Galway and the native Irish over a wide area. In the will of John Blake in 1468 are listed eighteen debtors who owed him just over 2,400 hides: only one is a stranger, from Bristol; the rest are native Irish. Not that the trade did anything to make the native Irish any more welcome in Galway: they were already excluded by a by-law of 1460, and probably by previous practice.

By and large, the fifteenth century seems to have been a period of steady prosperity for Galway, and the city was able to maintain sporadic contact with the government in Dublin. In the fifteenth century the Dublin government could do little

131

to help Galway, nor were successive Lancastrian kings much inclined to do so. With the accession of the Yorkist Edward IV in 1461, a king who was also heir to the lands and rights of the earldom of Ulster, the burgesses saw their chance and seized it: in 1464 they obtained a confirmation of their existing privileges, and to them was added the right to exclude from the town any person they chose, the lieutenant and chancellor of Ireland alone excepted – a right which could be exercised against the Clanricard Burkes, if the town were maintained in a sound state of defence. It marks an important step towards the full independence granted by the charter of 1484: by this, all earlier grants were confirmed, and the town was licensed to elect yearly a mayor and two bailiffs, as in Bristol. Without their permission, not even the lieutenant and chancellor of Ireland could enter the town, and Mac William Burke of Clanricard was explicitly excluded from any lordship over the town save by the consent of the mayor, bailiffs and corporation – not at all a likely eventuality. The first mayor and bailiffs were elected on 1 August 1485 and sworn into office at Michaelmas, 29 September.

At the same time the town gained control of the church within its walls – not that of the Franciscans, which had been on St Stephen's Island outside the north gate since William Liath de Burgo founded it in 1296, and which was the only friary until the Dominicans settled in 1488 more or less where they now are – but St Nicholas's itself. Since the establishment of a permanent vicarage in 1398 the burgesses were sure, in theory, of having their spiritual needs seen to; but not all vicars, whether appointed by Knockmoy or the bishop or the pope, had been entirely satisfactory. John Riss or Rice, appointed vicar of St Nicholas's about 1446, by his own admission had attempted to bribe the archbishop of Tuam – apparently successfully – to refrain from appointing anyone else to the vicarage in competition with him. He disappears from sight after being accused in 1455 of assault and bloodshed on a priest, of simony and perjury. And whatever about the personal integrity of subsequent vicars, there is ample evidence of confusion over who exactly were the legitimate holders of the vicarage.

It was obviously time for a thorough tidy-up, and in the year of the charter the burgesses persuaded Donatus Ó Muireadhaigh, archbishop of Tuam, to release jurisdiction over the vicarage to the town and to set up St Nicholas's as a collegiate church of eight vicars under a warden, who were to be presented and chosen only by the inhabitants of Galway; and they had this arrangement confirmed by Pope Innocent VIII. Once in full control of the church within the town, the municipality proceeded, with admirable briskness, to see to its upkeep by obtaining for it the revenues of near-by parishes. It already had the vicarage of Claregalway; in 1487 were added the rectory and vicarage of Oranmore and the vicarage of Maree, and in 1488 the vicarages of Rahoon and Moycullen; and stage by stage from then down to 1529 it received further benefices in Kinlaghan, Shrower and Roscam. In effect the collegiate church exercised jurisdiction over a respectable part of the area around Galway, and in turn the mayor and council of Galway exercised jurisdiction over the warden and vicars, even to the extent that they possessed the exclusive right to correct, control and punish the wardens and vicars; any complaint about them was to be made to the mayor and council, not the bishop or archbishop. Similarly, the town administered the college's property, saw to repairs, and levied toll on the town for the upkeep of the college.

The full independence gained in 1484 began a period, not only marked by rising wealth, heavily concentrated in the hands of the ruling families, the so-called Tribes of Galway – Lynches, Martins, Blakes and so on – but also demonstrated by the impressive stone buildings which replaced the dwellings destroyed in the great fire of 1473. The sixteenth century over-all was a time of prosperity, rarely disturbed: the citizenry's minds were concentrated on such things as the freeing of Galway, in 1544, from paying all customs, and its endowment with control of Galway Bay, rather than on Henry VIII's religious changes. These apparently bothered the people of Galway not at all: loyal to the king, they took the Oath of Supremacy acknowledging Henry as head of the Church, without changing their observance of the Catholic liturgy in St Nicholas's. They managed to maintain this for a full generation, until 1568 when the church was taken over by the reformers, and mass was thereafter celebrated in private houses. Of more concern were recurrent disruptions in the 1560s and 1570s by the unruly sons of the earl of Clanricard.

By the end of the sixteenth century, thanks to the grant in 1578 of further rights to the mayor and corporation of Galway, the city was close to being a statelet within the State – a very tolerant one, in which Catholic clergy moved freely and discreetly. Only towards the end are signs of decline visible, for reasons over which Galway had no control, and on which the erection of the city into a separate county in 1610 had no effect. What in the end put paid to its prosperity was less slow decline than the 1641 rising, in which Galway backed the royalists, and its suppression by the forces of Cromwell, ending in 1655 with orders to evacuate the papist inhabitants of the city, leaving it open to casual wrecking by Cromwellian soldiery. From that point on, it was an open question whether Galway would survive at all.

Select bibliography

M. J. Blake: *Blake Family Records*, i-ii, London, 1902–5.

M. J. Blake: 'The obituary book of the Franciscan monastery at Galway, 1485–1625', *Journal of the Galway Archaeological and Historical Society*, vi (1909–10), pp. 222–35; vii (1911–12), pp. 1–28.

J. Hardiman: *The History of the Town and County of the Town of Galway*, Dublin, 1820, reprinted Galway, 1975.

H. G. Leask: 'The collegiate church of St Nicholas, Galway', *Journal of the Galway Archaeological and Historical Society*, xvii (1936–7), pp 1–23.

S. Ó Catháin: 'Galway – "An ancient colonie of English"', *Studies*, xxxi (1942), pp. 456–66.

D. Ó Cearbhaill (ed.): *Galway: Town and Gown 1484–1984*, Dublin, 1984, chapters 1–3.

M. D. O'Sullivan: 'The lay school at Galway in the sixteenth and seventeenth centuries', *Journal of the Galway Archaeological and Historical Society*, xv (1931–3), pp. 1–32.

M. D. O'Sullivan: *Old Galway: the History of a Norman Colony in Ireland*, 2nd edition, Galway, 1983.

Galway in the Modern Period: Survival and Revival

Gearóid Ó Tuathaigh

THE progress in status that marked Galway's transition from the late medieval to the beginning of the early modern period was followed by a more turbulent experience during the late sixteenth and throughout the seventeenth century. The unsettled political conditions of the third quarter of the sixteenth century adversely affected the trade and prosperity of the city. During the early seventeenth century, however, the wealth of Galway citizens increased to such an extent that they were in a position to purchase lands in various parts of Connacht, in addition to their assets in Galway itself and its hinterland. Nevertheless the complex political and religious divisions that marked Ireland in the late sixteenth and early seventeenth century enveloped Galway, leading eventually to major convulsion in the mid-seventeenth century. The chief Galway families backed the royalist cause in the 1640s, and suffered for it when Cromwell and the Commonwealth prevailed. The surrender of Galway after a difficult siege was followed by a major destruction of the city, the expulsion of the leading Catholic interests, and the establishment of a new Protestant ruling oligarchy under Cromwellian dispensation. The atmosphere was poisoned by religious bitterness; the trade and physical appearance of the city had suffered great damage. The Restoration period saw only a minor Catholic 'revival', with very limited restoration of Catholic property, despite tolerance of

Prospect of Galway from the south-west c. 1820.

Lower Fairhill in the Claddagh, Galway, c. 1890.

Catholic worship and general trading in the city. The accession of James II further strengthened the Catholic interest in Galway, but with the 'war of the two kings' in 1689–91 the issue of who would hold power and privilege was finally settled, in Galway as elsewhere in Ireland, with the victory of William and Mary and of the Protestant cause.

The settlement that followed the final defeat of the Stuart cause at Aughrim resulted in the re-establishment of Protestant control in Galway, and in the sporadic application in the city during the early decades of the eighteenth century of some of the penal laws against Catholics. The few Jacobite scares up to 1745 prompted an excited but usually brief response among the Protestant oligarchy, with assertions of their power in the form of restrictions on Catholics within the walls, curfews, expulsions and some efforts at improving the security of the city's defences – fortifying the perimeter wall and ramparts. But these scares had all but died out by the 1740s and strictly religious interference (for example, the arrest of priests and friars) almost entirely lapsed, so that the Catholic population of the town grew significantly while the Protestant numbers remained low at several hundred.

The weakening of religious animosity, however, did not translate into an efficient administration or improved economic prosperity for Galway. On the contrary, the general neglect of the upkeep of the walls of the city from the middle of the eighteenth century merely reflected a deeper malaise and neglect in civic responsibility on the part of the self-perpetuating, self-serving clique who controlled the corporation of the city, enjoying all the perks and privileges that went with this political control. Ambitious or business-like merchants were reluctant to settle in the city. Traders and tradesmen were also burdened with obligations to the corporation. Not surprisingly, the trade and prosperity of the city declined in the middle decades of the century. It was especially ironic that, as Galway's prosperity (and its port traffic) declined, the business acumen of scions of leading Galway families was being exercised abroad, as Lynches, Kirwins, Bodkins, Blakes and others established an extraordinary network of trade and commerce in the West Indies, in Nantes, Bordeaux and other continental ports, as well as in Dublin and London. But at home in Galway, political intrigue seemed to absorb most of the energy of the ruling families. Occasional demands for 'reform' produced only limited amelioration of the worst excesses of corruption. The general body of the inhabitants of the city and surrounding area suffered, if not in silence, then certainly with remarkable patience.

Despite these adverse conditions, the pressure of the population growth and the general growth in the agricultural economy in Ireland in the closing decades of the eighteenth century did portend a period of change and of uneven development for Galway. By the turn of the century there was building on and outside the demolished old walls and fortifications; houses were built around Meyrick (later Eyre) Square, up Prospect Hill, and into Dominick Street on the western fringe of the city. As the new century began, some new buildings appeared within the old city, including a number of town houses for local gentry. However, population increase among the poorer classes was already producing heavy congestion and poverty in some of the older courtyard buildings. Indeed pre-Famine Galway presents us, as it presented contemporary observers, with a picture of contrasts and contradictions.

There were clear signs of development and progress. The new spacious County Infirmary opened its doors in 1802. Communications between the old city and its suburbs and hinterland improved in the pre-Famine decades. In 1831 a new bridge was completed on the west side of the city, linking the court house and the jail. In the next two decades the construction of the Clifden road opened up communications to the west and into Connemara, though land communications along the coastline of south Connemara remained poor, with the sea-route as the main link with the coastal communities until late in the century when, with State subvention, light railways finally (and, as it has proved, briefly) brought the more remote reaches of Connemara into the link with Galway and the national grid. But it is fair to say that improved communications contributed to the increasing volume of tourist traffic that headed west from Galway as the nineteenth century moved on. The general growth and increased visibility of the role of the State in the lives of the citizens, which was a feature of Ireland under the Union, is well illustrated in Galway. The new county jail opened its doors in June 1811, and four years later the court house was completed. With the establishment of a centralised police force in the 1830s, police barracks were the next formidable buildings attesting to the State's concern with law and order. No less formidable were the workhouses, constructed between 1839 and 1845, to provide grim institutional care for the destitute.

But the State infrastructure of care was not all custodial or coercive. The Commissioners of Public Works contributed to major construction works in Galway harbour in the 1830s. These harbour improvements were undoubtedly an incentive to increased traffic in the port in the decades that followed, but Galway port never quite succeeded in realising the high hopes of those who saw it as potentially a major trans-Atlantic port. Several attempts were made, notably in the late 1850s and early 1860s, to establish Galway as the eastern terminus for Atlantic mails, but such schemes were short-lived and unsuccessful.

A happier ending followed the demands that Galway be the western terminus for one of the major rail lines. The Midland Great Western Railway opened its line for traffic from Dublin to Galway on 1 August 1851. At the same time a splendid hotel was opened at the terminus in Galway. The coming of the railway had a considerable impact on Galway and its hinterland. The wholesale and retail trade and distribution systems were decisively changed by the railway. But the impact on passenger traffic was, perhaps, even more significant than on freight. The tourist traffic to the west was boosted considerably by the line, but on the other hand the railway also facilitated the growing outflow of emigrants, setting out from Galway with their third-class tickets in search of employment or a new future.

The second quarter of the nineteenth century saw significant developments in education in Galway and here, too, the role of the State was considerable. The establishment of the State system of elementary education in 1831 coincided and combined with the establishment of houses by religious orders of nuns (and later brothers), leading to new schools for the less affluent children of the city. The combined effect of these educational advances was gradually to reduce the figures for illiteracy (in the English language) throughout the century, so that by 1901 it was below 20 per cent in Galway city. More risky, perhaps, was the decision of Sir Robert Peel's government in 1845 to establish one of the new Queen's Colleges in Galway. The splendid stone quadrangular building (erected during the Famine years, 1846 to 1849) was an act of faith and of hope, and also, in a certain sense, of charity. Owing to the declared opposition of the Catholic hierarchy to the 'godless colleges', numbers attending the Queen's College remained low throughout the nineteenth century (though there was a healthy denominational mix among those attending), and the college was threatened with closure on several occasions up to the 1920s.

The expanding role of the State in early Victorian Ireland was powered, to a degree, by a reforming impulse. By the 1830s this reforming impulse confronted the complex, unrepresentative, and generally inadequate and venal structures of urban local government throughout Britain and Ireland. The Municipal Reform Act of 1840 brought major reforms in virtually all the established corporations in Ireland. The notoriously selfish and widely-criticised Galway Corporation was not reformed; it was abolished. Its passing was not greatly lamented by the citizens. Already a special board of twenty-four commissioners (elected under a restrictive property franchise) had been established by law, with responsibilities for looking after paving and lighting in the city. These were among the aspects of town government most neglected by the old corporation. John Barrow noted during his visit to Galway in the mid-1830s the 'narrow and dirty streets, and like the generality of the streets of the towns of Ireland, extremely ill-paved'. The commissioners clearly had a difficult task, yet by 1837 they had allowed a private company to provide gas street lighting and during the next fifteen years they saw to the paving of the streets and footpaths.

The reforming zeal of the 1830s did not stop at local government. In 1831 a long overdue reform of the organisation of the Catholic Church in Galway saw the abolition of the controversial (elected) office of warden and the establishment of a conventional diocese of Galway. The growth in the numbers and in the range of activities of Catholic priests, nuns and brothers has been one of the few unequivocally expansionist stories in Galway's history from the 1820s until relatively recent times. The pace of commercial life also quickened. By the late 1830s business interests in the town had formed themselves into a chamber of commerce, while the extension of joint-stock banking in the second quarter of the century saw Galway with branches of the Bank of Ireland, the Provincial and the National before 1850.

The numerous visitors to Galway in the pre-Famine years almost invariably remarked on the special character of the tightly knit and heavily populated Claddagh fishing village on the south-west margins of the old city. With a population as high, perhaps, as 6,000 on the eve of the Famine, the Claddagh's 'autonomy' from the city of Galway and the generally self-contained order of its life created a favourable, not to say romantic, impression among outside visitors. Yet it is worth reminding ourselves that the Claddagh in pre-Famine times endured its share of disease and suffering (including an outbreak of cholera in 1832), and that the fishing industry that supported its economy was generally judged to be most inefficient.

Indeed the general economic base of Galway in the mid-nineteenth century accounts for some of the contrasts and contradictions that struck many of the visitors to the city. The population of the municipal borough was above 17,000 by 1841, but that of the parliamentary borough of greater Galway (including parts of the parishes of Oranmore and Rahoon) was about 34,000. A huge pool of the chronically unemployed swamped the labour market and depressed wages.

Agriculture was the basis of Galway's pre-Famine economic activity – with numerous mills for grain, oatmeal and malt. Brewing and distilling, paper-making, tanning, iron-mongering and, most unusually, black marble fireplaces were the main manufactures, while the main port imports included timber, wine, salt, coal, hemp, tallow and iron. But the living conditions of the growing numbers of the poor and destitute were desperate, with outbreaks of typhus and relapsing fever and at least one visitation of cholera reaping a grim harvest in the pre-Famine years. The ravages of the Great Famine took a heavy toll in Galway. As disease-carrying and hungry paupers crowded into the city, the workhouse system and various schemes of food distribution and relief under government or voluntary charity auspices were simply overwhelmed. Emigration became a flood and mortality figures soared. By 1861 the population of the parliamentary borough had fallen back to c. 25,000, while that of the smaller municipal borough of Galway was just under 17,000. In the four decades that followed, the losses through emigration resulted in further decline in Galway's population.

	1861	1871	1901
Galway (parliamentary borough):	25,161	19,843	16,257
Galway (municipal borough):	c. 16,967	15,597	13,426

Changes in the economy and structure of employment in Galway between the Famine and the establishment of the Free State in 1922 were not dramatic. Nevertheless Galway was not immune to the general trend towards the creation of a more highly integrated wholesale and retail distribution network throughout the island, which was a feature of the railway age in Ireland. Local manufacturers, particularly in non-perishable goods, faced increased competition from cheap imports. Galway remained a crucial junction for wholesale distribution over a wide area of the west. Its own manufacturing base contracted, though not dramatically. The port remained a significant one for the west coast, with a steady coaster trade and a modest traffic in basic imports (timber, coal, iron and salt) and exports (agricultural products). The city's economy may have been sluggish, but improvements did take place in the lives of the citizens. The city had a comprehensive piped water supply by the late 1860s. The service sector generally experienced a growth in employment, as white-collar clerkships and shop assistants provided new opportunities. The army garrison and the various officers of the government boosted the State's service jobs. The Catholic Church was a spectacular growth area of the whitest of white-collar employment.

In terms of the general cultural ambience of the city, deference presided over much of the gentry-sponsored social events. Perhaps the most significant cultural change in the city was the spread of English as a vernacular from the small core of the city itself in the eighteenth century in an ever-widening radius as the nineteenth century moved on. Yet, despite the growing wedge of English-speaking Galway, the sheer ubiquity of Irish-speakers on all sides of the city meant that more Irish was to be heard on the streets of Galway (if not necessarily in the shops) at the turn of the century than in any other Irish city. The most notable social change was the growth in popularity of the suburb of Salthill as a bathing and seaside resort, where a growing number of spacious houses were built for visitors, and which the citizens of Galway increasingly saw as a recreation area for walks and bathing.

Deference was also the key to the long political hegemony of the old Galway landlord families in the parliamentary representation of the borough up to the 1880s, until the Parnellite machine dictated that 'loyalty to party and to the nationalist cause' should prevail over local loyalties and pedigree in Galway elections. The number of those eligible to vote remained small (2,320 voters out of a total population of *c*. 16,000 in the Galway City constituency in 1911), but the general political disposition of the citizens seemed relaxed, as evidenced by the communal welcome given to Edward VII on his visit to Galway in 1903. Nevertheless the rise of cultural nationalism, together with the revival of more separatist nationalism, affected the political temper of Galway at the turn of the century, eventually producing recruits for the 'new nationalism' that launched the 1916 rising, swept Sinn Féin to electoral victory, and led to the founding of Dáil Éireann in 1919 and of the Irish Free State in 1922.

The first decades of the Irish Free State brought steadily improving fortunes to Galway. Status increased with the restoration of the mayoral dignity and corporation in 1937. The role of the State was crucial. The housing stock of the ordinary workers was improved by the construction of new public housing in Shantalla, Bohermore and the Claddagh. The population of the city increased steadily from 14,227 in 1926, to 21,366 in 1956, and to 23,700 in 1961. The most notable feature of the changing economic and employment profile was the growth in service sector employment, relative to other categories. Manufacturing employment almost doubled (to 1,427) in the period 1911–61, but from a low base. The protectionist régime from the 1930s, in particular, encouraged some new jobs in electrical goods, chemicals and concrete, metal- and woodwork; but textiles, clothing and footwear experienced losses in employment. In any case, the manufacturing share of employment moved only between 16 and 19 per cent throughout the period, compared to the 65 to 71 per cent share for the service sector. Holiday traffic to Salthill boosted tourism as a major factor in Galway's economy.

In healthcare and education there was steady progress. In health the principal post-war programme culminated in the opening of Merlin Park Sanatorium in 1953–4 and of the new Regional Hospital in 1956. In addition to these, the early 1950s saw the opening of Calvary Private Hospital by the Little Company of Mary. The numbers attending University College (a college of the National University of Ireland since 1908) gradually increased from the 1920s to the early 1960s, when it exceeded 1,000 for the first time. The influence of State policy was also felt in other, more unusual, ways. In the policy for the revival of the Irish language as the main vernacular, Galway (with its strong Irish-speaking hinterland) was seen as having a crucial part to play: an Irish-language theatre – An Taibhdhearc – was established with State support in 1928, an Irish-speaking battalion was stationed in the garrison at Renmore, and in 1929 University College Galway was given a special role in providing university courses through Irish.

The most spectacular phase of growth in Galway's modern history, however, dates from the 1960s. The strategy of identifying and concentrating on a number of key centres for investment that followed the general national policy shift on economic development and planning (with, for a time, a regional dimension) from the late 1950s and through the 1960s, and specifically the identification of Galway in the Buchanan Report of 1968 as one of the six key regional centres with potential for industrial growth, heralded the spectacular development of the city that has occurred during the past thirty years. The establishment of an industrial estate in Mervue in 1966; the choice of Galway as the regional headquarters of the Western Health Board in 1971; the establishment of a new third-level educational institution (the Regional Technical College) in 1972, and the growth in student numbers in University College (from *c.* 1,900 in 1964 to *c.* 7,000 in 1994); together with continued expansion in the general infrastructure and facilities of the tourist industry and a broadly expansionist service sector; finally a strong education-technology base to industrial development – these are but the key elements of a success story that has seen the population of Galway rise from 24,517 in 1966 to 37,835 in 1981, and further to 50,800 in 1991.

The development role of Udarás na Gaeltachta in the Gaeltacht hinterland and the generally more up-beat story of the Irish language cultural and communications grid have provided the incentive for a more assertive presence for Irish in the civic and business life of the city. At the same time there has been a remarkable explosion of arts activities and creativity in Galway since the 1960s. Cynics remark that Galway's public calendar seems to consist of a long list of festivals and sporting events. The renaissance in the arts has been all the more remarkable in view of the relatively under-developed physical infrastructure for major artistic events in the city. Indeed, while the physical evidence of the city's growth is striking (with housing developments stretching to all extremities of the city's limits and beyond, with large shopping malls on both the east and the west side and with considerable renewal in the heart of the old city), the appropriateness, in style and scale, of some of the city centre development is open to question.

The revitalisation of the heart of the old city for social and leisure life has, to some extent, been at the expense of Salthill, which finds itself in the changing summer leisure culture of Ireland in the 1990s having to consider carefully its role and future prospects. This is also the case for the country towns within the effective 'consumer radius' (c. 25 miles) of Galway. Galway's boom as a shopping, leisure, service and educational centre has sucked some of the lifeblood from these towns and, indeed, from the rural communities in parts of its hinterland. The continued growth of Galway as a major regional centre will pose further challenges, both for those living in the city and for those living in the catchment area. It is undeniable, however, that as Galway moves towards the new millennium its problems and challenges are those generated by success, growth and development. From an historical perspective it is likely that the final third of the twentieth century will count among the most confident and expansionist episodes in the long history of the western capital.

Select bibliography

M. Coen: *The Wardenship of Galway*, Galway, 1984.

J. Cunningham: *Labour in the West of Ireland*, Belfast, 1995.

T. de Bhaldraithe (ed.): *Seanchas Thomáis Laighléis*, Dublin, 1977.

J. Hardiman: *The History of the Town and County of the Town of Galway*, Dublin, 1820, reprinted Galway, 1975.

J. P. Murray: *Galway: a Medico-social History*, Galway, 1994.

S. Ní Chinnéide: 'Coquebert de Montbret's impressions of Galway city and county in the year 1791', *Journal of the Galway Archaeological and Historical Society*, xxv (1952–3), pp. 1–14.

D. Ó Cearbhaill (ed.): *Galway: Town and Gown 1484–1984*, Dublin, 1984.

N. P. T. O'Donnellan: 'Manufacturing Industry in Galway 1911–57', unpublished M.A. thesis, University College Galway, 1979.

M. D. O'Sullivan: *Old Galway: the History of a Norman Colony in Ireland*, 2nd edition, Galway, 1983.

M. Semple: *Some Galway Memories: a Pictorial Record*, revised edition, Galway, 1990.

The former market cross, High Street, Kilkenny.

Rothe House, Kilkenny.

150

KILKENNY – THE FAIRE CITIE

John Bradley

VISITORS to our town [wrote James Delehanty in 1970] *are usually enchanted with it. The more sophisticated they are the greater their delight. Here, set in the heart of a smiling countryside, on the banks of a beautiful unspoilt river, stands this Norman city of the Pale, stone-built and solid, abounding in picturesque corners and alleyways, steps, arches, walls, gables, dominated by its castle and ... cathedral, inhabited by some ten thousand people of mixed Irish and Norman stock combining the qualities of those two great strains, friendly, though not without malice, intelligent, witty and often cynical, capable of considerable achievement, if a trifle indolent withal.*

Kilkenny's ability to enchant is perhaps its most long-lived tradition. From almost the moment when visitors began to record impressions it has elicited favourable notices. Richard Stanihurst, for instance, writing in 1584 described it as:

a beautiful town. It occupies a prime site and its air is free from harmful vapours. It has a noble river, the Nore, which never freezes in wintertime. The river-bank gardens are continuously irrigated by pure subterranean streams. Kilkenny is noted for its fine buildings and, more importantly, for its honest townspeople.

To Fynes Moryson, writing in 1600, it was 'the chief of all the towns within land, memorable for the civility of its inhabitants'. Dr John Bale, remembered today as the first historian of English literature, also praised the character of the townspeople and, despite the trauma of his subsequent eviction, Kilkenny remained for him 'a civile town', and was the only Irish town to which he ascribed that adjective in his autobiographical tract of 1553. In the seventeenth century French and Italian visitors drew comparisons with the towns of their home countries while David Rothe, admittedly a native son, was so enraptured by Kilkenny's wealth and growth that he suggested it was time it was renamed in classical style, Canicopolis.

It was, however, Edmund Spenser who had the most enduring impact. He visited Kilkenny at least twice, in 1580 and again in 1581. In the *Faerie Queene* he was moved to write of:

> ... *the stubborn Newre whose waters gray*
> *By faire Kilkenny and Rosseponte boord.*

Whether or not he was the first to describe Kilkenny as 'faire' is unclear, but the adjective was applied soon after and, as 'the faire citie', it became Kilkenny's motto. It appears every week beneath the city arms on the masthead of *The Kilkenny People*, where the letters *The* are still spelt *Ye*, following the seventeenth-century scribal practice of denoting the sound *th* with a letter resembling *y*.

Kilkenny's period of importance, during which it was celebrated as 'the faire citie', lasted a little over a century from about 1520 until 1650. This was the period when the Butler family, reinstated once more as earls, devoted their attention to the development of Kilkenny, importing Flemish weavers, founding a famous school, and stylishly patronising the arts, as their splendid tombs in St Canice's Cathedral and the Holbein portrait in the Royal Collection at Windsor testify. It was not just nobility, however, who devoted themselves to the city. The late sixteenth century was a time of commercial prosperity for Kilkenny and it was ruled by an oligarchy, composed of rich merchant families who, between them, controlled every office of Church and State that Kilkenny had to offer. Their family names were so well known that they have come down to us as a jingle:

Archdekin, Archer, Cowley, Langton, Lee,
Knaresborough, Lawless, Raggett, Rothe and Shee.

It was the efforts of politically astute individuals within these families that secured, in 1609, the elevation of Kilkenny from town to city. And it was these ten families who built the great stone houses that gave Kilkenny its reputation and whose remnants, like Rothe House, saved from official neglect and entrepreneurial greed, still have the power to enchant today. The inspiration behind this extraordinary civic architecture was provided by a man who stands over this period like a colossus. He was Thomas Butler, tenth earl of Ormond, and known to posterity because of his dark hair as Black Tom. He was equally at home in Kilkenny and at the court of Queen Elizabeth, and he had connections at the heart of the English Renaissance. Spenser addressed one of the dedicatory verses of the *Faerie Queene* to him, while another poet, Philip Sidney, famously lost control of his words in a dispute with Black Tom. The earl spent his life moving back and forth between Kilkenny, Dublin and London, and the influences were not simply all one way. It is Black Tom's court that provides the most likely medium through which the song *Cailín Óg cois tSúire mé* reached London, where it was to be transcribed by John Dowland and used as a popular catchphrase by Shakespeare in his play *Henry V*. But the influence of the English Renaissance is nowhere more clearly seen than in the architecture of the manor-house at Carrick-on-Suir, built by Black Tom in 1565. Here, for the first time in Ireland, was a revolutionary building emphasising space, light and domestic warmth. It was this building, more than any other, which provided the inspiration for the civic architecture that Stanihurst praised and that gave Kilkenny its epithet of 'faire'. The seventeenth-century city, however, did not simply emerge out of nowhere. In fact, a millennium of growth had occurred by the time Kilkenny acquired its status as a city.

The key factor in Kilkenny's success was undoubtedly its geographical situation. Located beside a fording point on the River Nore, the site is a nodal point within the small central plain that forms the fertile heartland of County Kilkenny. The city is focused on a meander and the ground rises gradually on both sides of the river. The name *Cill Chainnigh*, 'Canice's church', provides clear evidence of the settlement's origin as an Early Christian centre dedicated to St Canice. Three ancient lives of Canice survive, but they contain little in the way of either historical information or spiritual edification. Their principal value lies in the fact that they preserve the tradition that Canice was descended from the Ciannachta Duine Geimhin (County Derry) and they show a close relationship between Canice's foundations and the monasteries founded by Columba and Comgall. Little can be said of Canice himself with any certainty. According to the *Annals of Ulster* he died in 599 or 600 and a date for his *floruit* in the second half of the sixth century is unlikely to be far wrong.

It is possible that Canice founded Kilkenny in person, but very little is known about the way in which early Irish monasteries received their dedications and it is at least as likely that it was established at a later stage by one of his disciples. Canice's principal foundation in southern Ireland was at Aghaboe, County Laois, and it is normally referred to as *Cill Chainnigh* or *Cill Mór Chainnigh* in the annals. The use of the same place-name for both Aghaboe and Kilkenny can lead to confusion and accordingly it is difficult to know exactly when the annalists stop referring to Aghaboe and begin to refer to Kilkenny.

Kilkenny's rise to prominence was an indirect result of Viking activity in southern Ireland. Traditionally the Osraige, within whose territory Kilkenny was located, were one group of a Munster people known as the Érainn. They occupied an intermediate position between Munster and Leinster, and, in the centuries between 500 and 800, were essentially a buffer between the two great provinces. In the mid-ninth century, however, because of the emergence of a powerful and ambitious king, Osraige developed aspirations of controlling Leinster itself. The king was Cerball mac Dúnlainge (died 888) who, as *Kjarval Irakonungr* ('Kjarvall the Irish king'), was subsequently remembered in the genealogies of some of the leading Icelandic families. His success was due in large measure to two factors: firstly, a skill in manipulating rival bands of Vikings by a combination of diplomacy and marriage alliances; secondly, his military prowess – an ability to defeat them in battle when necessary. The Viking presence gave a new dimension to Irish waterways and the Nore and Barrow, reaching some 40 miles into the interior of Ireland, became major arteries of communication. Cerball's success was founded on his domination of the river valleys and, during the 870s and 880s, this made him the most powerful king in Leinster.

The relevance of Cerball mac Dúnlainge's rise to prominence, and that of his Mac Gilla Patraic successors, lies in the fact that their lands, the fertile plain of central Kilkenny, became the centre of power in Osraige. Centrally placed within these lands and overlooking the River Nore, the monastery at Kilkenny had a locational significance that was not shared by the more remote, even if more famous, Sierkieran and Aghaboe. This shift in power, which commenced in the late ninth century and was consolidated in the tenth and eleventh centuries, effectively marks Kilkenny's beginnings as a town.

The church dedicated to Canice was established on a hill overlooking the major fording point of the Nore beside Green's Bridge. Nothing is known of the form of the early church, but examination of the modern street pattern suggests that it stood within a large enclosure, similar to other large monasteries such as Armagh and Kells (County Meath). The former existence of this enclosure is indicated by the curving alignment of Vicar Street, St Canice's Place and Dean Street. In the absence of archaeological excavation, little can be said of what existed within this area. A stone church is known to have stood here prior to the coming of the Anglo-Normans because about a dozen stones decorated in Hiberno-Romanesque style have been found on the site. The round tower most likely dates to the eleventh century, but it was built on top of an earlier cemetery containing the burials of both adults and children. The discovery in the last century of antler tines near the cathedral suggests the presence of some form of manufacturing activity, such as antler-working or the comb-making that was carried out in contemporary centres such as Dublin and Kildare.

By the twelfth century the Mac Gilla Patraic kings of Ossory had a house here, in which they held court, and in which a 'seneschal' deputised during their absence. The location of this building can now be identified because excavation work by the archaeologist Ben Murtagh has recently uncovered parts of a pre-Norman structure on the site of the present Kilkenny Castle. Although the evidence is slight, it suggests that pre-Norman Kilkenny was not simply a religious settlement but also a centre of local administration and a place where craftwork was carried out. Its status is evidently reflected in the fact that after the Anglo-Norman invasion St Canice's became the centre of a separate borough, significantly called the Irishtown. Even in the late sixteenth century, as Stanihurst tells us, its burgesses retained the tradition that Irishtown was the older settlement, and it is in the persistent squabbling between the corporations of Irishtown and the Hightown (or Englishtown) of Kilkenny that the origin of the nickname 'Kilkenny cats' is to be found and not in the tall tale (if I may be excused the pun) of bored militia men amusing themselves by tying cats together over a clothes line. In any event, by 1169, when the first Anglo-Normans visited Kilkenny and were put up in its inns or *ostels*, as they called them, Kilkenny had already become the largest and most important settlement in the county.

The Anglo-Normans, however, transformed the town. Strongbow, the leader of the Anglo-Norman adventurers, retained the fertile lands of Kilkenny for himself and settlers had already begun to arrive before his death in 1176. It was his successor William Marshal who was to have the most profound effect on the development of the town. The initial Anglo-Norman town was established below the castle, which was taken over from the Mac Gilla Patraics and rebuilt. By the time Marshal visited the town in 1207 there was already a shortage of space for the settlers and so he negotiated the transfer of land between the River Bregagh and James's Street from the bishop of Ossory. This new area, on either side of the present Parliament Street, was probably settled between 1207 and *c.* 1225, when the Franciscan friary was founded in the north-east angle of the town.

The new thirteenth-century town was laid out along a single street, High Street, which ran northwards towards St Canice's Cathedral, from just below the castle as far as the boundary with Irishtown. At its southern end High Street intersected with Patrick Street, Castle Street (now The Parade) and Rose Inn Street, forming a junction which became known in the later Middle Ages as Crocker's Cross. High Street, as every motorist knows, is broader in the middle than at either end, and this careful design was devised so that it could accommodate a row of stalls on market day.

Some of the properties along High Street and Parliament Street (the relatively modern name of the northern end of the medieval High Street) still preserve the long narrow burgage plots characteristic of medieval towns throughout western Europe. Along the west side of High Street these plots stretched back uniformly from the street frontage as far as the town wall. These regularly arranged plots were the backbone of the Anglo-Norman town plan and William Marshal's foundation charter of 1207 stipulated that they should be 20 feet (6.1 metres) wide. Each of these plots was held by a burgess and on it he built a house for his family, perhaps with a shop on the street frontage, and behind it there was space for outhouses, sheds, herb gardens or an orchard.

Kilkenny also expanded on the east and south. An Augustinian monastery was founded on the east bank of the Nore and a settlement, known simply as St John's, grew up in its vicinity along the present John Street during the thirteenth century. On the south side of the town, in the neighbourhood of St Patrick's Church, was the borough of Donaghmore, first referred to *c*. 1250. It was presumably an extramural settlement based around St Patrick's Church, which itself is probably of pre-Norman date. Flemingstown also appears to have been outside the town, but its precise location has never been established.

The castle was one of the most important components in the Anglo-Norman town. Established before 1173, probably as a motte-and-bailey castle, it has played a critical role in the affairs of the town into modern times. The present stone structure belongs mainly to the thirteenth century and it was built by the Marshals. Subsequently Kilkenny Castle passed to the De Clares and Le Dispensers, before being sold to James Butler, third earl of Ormond, in 1391. It remained in the hands of the Butler family until 1969 when it was taken over by the State. In recent years it has been the subject of a magnificent restoration carried out by the Office of Public Works.

The pre-Norman cathedral of St Canice became the nucleus of the new borough of Irishtown or of 'the cross', as it was termed. The present building was begun in the early years of the thirteenth century and it remains one of the finest medieval churches in Ireland, showing a remarkable unity of design, despite the fact that it took some eighty years to build. Just as St Canice's functioned as the parish church of Irishtown, so St Mary's was the parish church of the Hightown, but there were at least three other churches that formed part of the parochial network: St Patrick's, itself a parish church, and the chapels of St Maul and St Rioc. The remains of St Mary's, now in use as a parish hall, show that it was a sizeable church possessing a chancel, transepts and an aisled nave. It was already in existence before 1206. Nothing survives of the medieval St Patrick's, but the series of thirteenth- and fourteenth-century tomb-slabs in the churchyard leaves one in no doubt about its importance in Anglo-Norman times.

The Augustinian priory of St John the Evangelist was founded c. 1211. None of the surviving remains, however, with the possible exception of the chancel's north wall, date to this time. The magnificent east window consisting of two triple lights probably dates to about the middle of the thirteenth century, while the lady chapel, once known from the continuous run of windows in its south wall as the 'lantern of Ireland', was built about 1280 at much the same time as the lady chapel of St Canice's Cathedral, to which it displays clear stylistic affinities.

The Dominican friary, popularly known as the Black Abbey, was founded c. 1225 by William Marshal the Younger. The long chancel, which stretched eastwards as far as Bridge Street, was demolished by the friars in the late eighteenth century in order to provide building stone for the present monastery. The choir and bell-tower of the Franciscan friary, together with a small fragment of the conventual buildings, still survive within Smithwick's Brewery. The medieval friary lay within a precinct occupying the north-eastern corner of the Hightown, bounded on the north by the River Bregagh and on the east by the Nore. The founder appears to have been Richard Marshal, who died in 1234.

The exact foundation date of the hospital of St Mary Magdalen, which was situated in Maudlin Street, is unclear but it was in existence by 1327 when it is first referred to. The Maudlin Castle still survives, albeit isolated in a forest of houses, but an old engraving shows that it protected a gate leading into the hospital enclosure that included the present St Stephen's churchyard within its bounds.

It is clear from this recitation of churches, monasteries and a hospital that the thirteenth century was a formative period in Kilkenny's growth. By contrast the fourteenth century was a period of decline. Building projects faltered, the extramural suburbs shrank or were abandoned and the population of the town was devastated in 1348 by the Black Death. There were some signs of economic recovery in the fifteenth century, but it was not until the middle of the sixteenth century that the town began to expand once again. The reasons for this have been outlined already, but it is evident that the sixteenth-century developers were building on a strong and old foundation.

The story of Kilkenny after its capture by Oliver Cromwell in 1650 is usually viewed as one of decline, but this is only partly true. The continued rise of Dublin and Waterford in the years after 1660 meant that Kilkenny never had the same economic importance as before; and it was never again the political nerve-centre that it had been during the short-lived Confederation of Kilkenny. In the course of the eighteenth century it took on the role of a quiet county town where revellers and gentry passed the time at balls or in taverns, epitomised by the Hole-in-the-Wall:

If you ever go to Kilkenny,
Remember the Hole-in-the-Wall,
You get blind drunk there for a penny,
And tipsy for nothing at all.

The eighteenth century, however, also saw the development of new industries. Milling became important and several breweries and distilleries were attracted to the town because of the quality of its water. Smithwick's Brewery, the oldest of these, was established in 1710. By 1841 the population of Kilkenny was over 20,000, but in the succeeding half-century this was to be depleted by famine and emigration to half that number, a figure at which it more or less still remains a century and a half later.

The worst effects of the industrial revolution passed Kilkenny by. The townspeople simply did not have the money to demolish the old seventeenth-century structures and so it was that they survived into our own time. In the past twenty years, however, more of these buildings have been destroyed than at any time since the visitation of Cromwell while, on the other hand, wonderful restorations have been carried out at Rothe House and the Shee Almshouse. How, then, stands 'the faire citie'?

> *And every fair* [says Shakespeare]
> *from fair sometimes declines,*
> *By chance, or nature's changing course untrimm'd;*
> *But thy eternal summer shall not fade …*

Well of course it may, because the 'fairness' of Kilkenny lies not just in its buildings, nor in the civility of its inhabitants (which I am glad to say is still there), but in something much more intangible. When Francis MacManus was asked what it was he liked most about Kilkenny he said:

> *The dearest thing I know is a memory of sunny Sunday mornings in Kilkenny: the lovely line of castle, roof-top, spire and round tower against the pale blue sky; the sun revelling in the quiet colours of old stone, old walls, old trees; the tip-tap of the feet of people on the flagstones, and above all, the flocking floating notes of the church bells. Sunday has a flavour all its own there, a clean, sweet, warming flavour.*

It would be easy to let this comment slip by as a nostalgic recollection, but it contains, I think, a profound insight. It says in more poetic words what I have been trying to communicate in this essay, that Kilkenny *is* a Renaissance city: it is all about light, space and intimacy. And if Kilkenny is to capitalise on the tourist Mecca that it has now become, then future developments must be carried out with great care and insight. With Renaissance insight, in fact!

Select bibliography

J. Bradley: 'The town wall of Kilkenny', *Old Kilkenny Review*, new series, i, no. 2 (1975), pp. 85–103; no. 3 (1976), pp. 209–18.

W. Carrigan: *The History and Antiquities of the Diocese of Ossory*, iii, Dublin, 1905, reprinted Kilkenny, 1981.

J. Delehanty: 'The Fair City', *The Kilkenny Magazine*, xviii (autumn–winter 1970), pp. 71–6.

A. Empey (ed.): *A Worthy Foundation: the Cathedral Church of St Canice, Kilkenny*, Mountrath, 1985.

J. Graves: 'Ancient street architecture in Kilkenny', *Journal of the Royal Society of Antiquaries of Ireland*, i (1849–51), pp. 41–7.

J. Hogan: *Kilkenny*, Kilkenny, 1884.

K. M. Lanigan and G. Tyler: *Kilkenny: its Architecture and History*, Kilkenny, 1977.

B. Murtagh: 'The Kilkenny Castle archaeological project 1990–93: interim report', *Old Kilkenny Review*, new series, iv, no. 5 (1993), pp. 1101–17.

W. G. Neely: *Kilkenny: an Urban History, 1391–1843*, Belfast, 1989.

W. Nolan and K. Whelan (eds): *Kilkenny: History and Society*, Dublin, 1990.

MEDIEVAL LIMERICK: THE GROWTH OF TWO TOWNS

Celie O'Rahilly

ONE wonders what Limerick might have looked like in the early medieval period. We can only imagine an island on the east bank of the Shannon: its tidal location at the head of the estuary, some 60 miles from the open sea, and its proximity to the Curragour Falls meant that it was used as a crossing point. The island, later known as the King's Island, is formed by the Abbey River that separates from the Shannon above the falls and rejoins it further south. This, combined with the low ground to the east, rendered it an area capable of being easily defended. The southern end of the island is elevated and it was, presumably, here that settlement first occurred.

The historical sources refer to a church, possibly a monastic-type settlement, founded by St Munchin in the sixth century. The site of this foundation is unknown, the only indication being the present-day St Munchin's Church, located just north of Thomond Bridge. It is contrary to our understanding of the situation to imagine this monastery or church co-existing with the Viking settlers. The survival of this church may have been due to its relative lack of wealth, or perhaps it was abandoned and only later revived following the establishment of the Scandinavian settlement and the conversion of its inhabitants, when the early church was used as their cathedral.

The initial incursions of the Viking fleets up the estuary occurred in the early ninth century. While there is no evidence that they used the island, its location on the river and its inaccessibility from the land must have made it a suitable base and

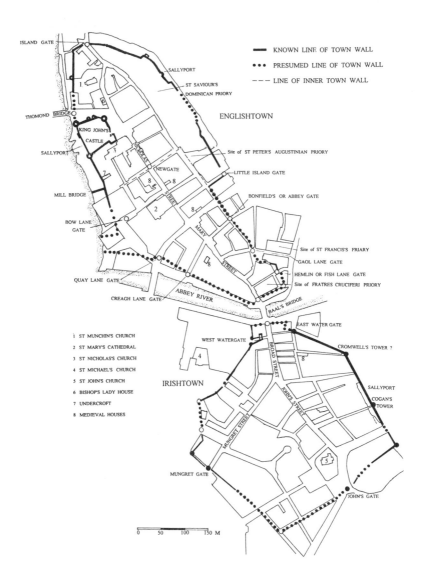

Map of Limerick showing the line of the medieval walls, the location of medieval buildings and surviving medieval remains.

led to some occupation. The Abbey River could have been used as a by-pass around the falls. It was a hundred years, however, before a permanent settlement was established under Tamar, a Norse king who was a rival to the king in Dublin. From the island it was possible both to carry out raids up the Shannon basin and to control the Atlantic trade. The location of this settlement can be identified only from negative evidence. We know from the sites that have been excavated or investigated to date where it was not, since none has produced any Viking or Hiberno-Norse deposits. Thus it is more by a process of elimination that the location of the Viking and later Hiberno-Norse settlement can be placed in the area centred around St Mary's Cathedral.

Until sites in this area are excavated, there is very little to be said regarding the layout or economy of the early Scandinavian settlement. Only by comparison with Dublin and Waterford can we presume that it was enclosed by a bank and ditch. There have been some isolated Viking finds from the vicinity of Limerick and references in the annals to its Vikings are numerous. The district seems to have remained for some fifteen years in the control of the Limerick Vikings as a separate kingdom and was subjected to Dublin rule only following their defeat at Lough Ree in 937. It was ruled by Dublin until 967 when the settlement was taken over by the Ua Briain, after which time the Hiberno-Norse town emerged.

It is possible, even from the lack of excavated evidence, to reconstruct an albeit vague picture of the outline of the Hiberno-Norse town, which probably followed the limits of St Mary's parish. The present Nicholas Street and Mary Street extend approximately north-south along the highest ground in the vicinity and form the backbone of the thoroughfare known as the High Street. It connects Thomond Bridge, crossing the Shannon, with Baal's Bridge over the Abbey River and its alignment is not likely to have differed at that time. The town

Pictorial map of Limerick c. 1590, detail showing the Irishtown.

166

may have been surrounded by a wall at the time of the arrival of the Anglo-Normans. The Civil Survey of 1654 notes several properties whose limits are specified as being formed by the town wall. These properties, when plotted on the Ordnance Survey plan of 1840, were located along Bishop Street, which runs parallel to and east of the High Street, and also on Francis Street, which links these two streets. The cartographic evidence shows Newgate on the High Street where it meets Francis Street and clearly depicted on the Hardiman map, dated traditionally to 1590, is a wall continuing to the Shannon along Newgate Lane. This line also coincides with the northern limit of St Mary's parish. That knowledge of this inner town wall survived to 1654 is not easily explained, since the subsequent walling of the area to the north as far as the Island Gate would have taken place after the arrival of the Anglo-Normans some 450 years prior to the Civil Survey.

The domination by the Ua Briain and their loss of control of the high-kingship meant that Limerick became the seat of control of Munster. In 1101 Muirchertach Ua Briain, having donated his palace at Cashel to the Church, moved to Limerick and, according to tradition, built his palace on the site of the Viking Thingmót. Ten years later, in 1111, the synod of Ráith Bressail presided over by Gilbert, the bishop of Limerick, defined the limits of the diocese and recognised St Mary's as its cathedral: *is é Teampall Muire i Luimneuch a prímheaglais*. This early cathedral church must originally have been located elsewhere: if the present St Mary's was the site of the king's palace in 1101, it is unlikely to have been a cathedral ten years later given that Domnall Mór Ua Briain donated the site to the Church only in 1194. The present structure underwent several building stages. Excavation here in 1992 proved that the west end, previously thought to be the earliest part of the building, dates in fact to the late thirteenth or early fourteenth century owing to the presence of burials with associated pottery that underlie the west wall. The Romanesque doorway must be from an earlier building that was located further east.

The extent of the Hiberno-Norse town can therefore be seen as occupying the southern end of the island defined to the west and south by the Shannon and Abbey Rivers respectively, to the north by the wall along Newgate Lane and Francis Street, and to the east by the wall extending parallel to the High Street along Bishop Street and Sheep Street, enclosing an area approximately 14½ acres in extent. At what stage the walls were built is a matter of conjecture, but it seems from a twelfth-century description that Limerick was a fortified stronghold with gates, towers and houses. The exact limit along the Abbey River is also uncertain. When one considers the subsequent incorporation of the religious foundations within the walled area, the probability is that the original south wall of the town was located further north.

As was commonly the case in the Middle Ages religious foundations were granted land outside the walled town. The first of these at Limerick was a gift by Domnall Mór Ua Briain in 1172 to the new Augustinian priory for nuns. This foundation, dedicated to St Peter, was located near the north-eastern angle of the existing town wall, and is still referred to as St Peter's Cell. Later foundations during the Anglo-Norman period lay on either side of this. The Hiberno-Norse town had laid down patterns for the future.

The success of the Anglo-Normans' conquest in Munster centred on their ability to establish a hold on the town and to retain it in the name of the reigning English monarch. Although this did not in itself lead to control *per se*, it at least provided a foothold in a region that since the death of Brian Bóruma had seen almost continuous feuding between Irish chieftains striving for kingship of the region or high-kingship of the country. Initially this control was chequered: in 1172 Domnall Mór submitted to King Henry II by allowing in a garrison; in 1176 Raymond le Gros entrusted the town to the guardianship of Ua Briain who, as soon as the garrison had left, burnt it and took it over.

The sequence of occupation of the castle revealed by the recent excavations there showed that, at the initial stages, the castle bawn was much smaller and was defended on the southern side by a massive ditch with an internal bank that was later revetted with dry-stone walling. The construction by the Anglo-Normans of a well-defended, strategically placed fortification must have been a matter of some urgency. Whether this resembled a motte-and-bailey is impossible to say, given its subsequent total eradication by the stone castle. This ditch does not appear to have remained open for long, since it was infilled not just with debris but also with lines of post-and-wattle that may have been property boundaries, implying that the ditch's use as a defensive element was short-lived. Post-dating the initial infill was the construction of a row of three sunken structures aligned north-south. The proximity of the ditch to the northernmost one would suggest that by the time of their construction the ditch was redundant. The resemblance of these sunken structures to ones found in Hiberno-Norse contexts Dublin and Waterford is striking, but the associated finds and stratigraphy put the building of the Limerick examples in the late twelfth century – that period in the town's history, from 1176 to 1196, when it had reverted to Irish control.

Despite the speculative grant of Limerick to Philip de Braose in 1177, it was not until after the death of Domnall Mór Ua Briain in 1194 that the Anglo-Normans regained any effective control of the town. William de Burgo, having married Domnall Mór's daughter in 1193, gained some ground in Munster and by 1196 the town was again held by the Anglo-Normans – a situation that was ratified by the charter of the Lord John in the following year. In 1201 the Lord John, who by then had become the king of England, granted William de Braose the honour of Limerick, but retained the lands of De Burgo, the Englishtown (as it can now be called), the church-land and the cantred of the Ostmen. Between 1203 and 1210 there were various transfers of control between the Anglo-Normans – among them two of the justiciars or chief governors of the developing colony in Ireland, Meiler fitz Henry and John de Grey – and it was during this period that the construction of the royal castle in stone must have taken place.

An entry in the *Black Book* of Limerick is an order by John that post-dates 1199 when he became king and pre-dates 1210 when he arrived in Ireland, prohibiting the building of a castle on lands owned by Bishop Donnchad Ua Briain. This means that the castle had to be built beyond the parish boundary not just of St Mary's, but also of St Nicholas's, immediately north of Newgate, because that land, too, belonged to the bishop. Practical considerations – such as the location of the earlier fortification, the suitability of the site close to the river crossing, and the relatively high ground compared to the surrounding area – no doubt contributed to this choice of site.

The initial stone castle consisted of the north-east and north-west towers, with an entrance, later modified, all linked by a curtain wall that continued south from the north-east tower. Its southern end was built against the stone-revetted earthen embankment mentioned earlier, which therefore continued to serve as the southern limit of the defences. The Shannon formed a natural boundary to the west. A pipe roll entry of 1212 records the expenditure of £733 16s. 11d. on the castle. This could be interpreted as payment for the construction of the stone castle, since we may reasonably assume that such payment would have been made on completion of the work.

By the mid-1220s the castle had apparently fallen into a state of neglect, for in 1227 a clerk was sent from Dublin to make the castle habitable and suitable for use as a mint and exchequer. It is possible that the beginning of the extension southwards of the bawn, which was done in stages, dates to this period. From the excavated evidence it seems that the first stage was the digging of a ditch and internal bank around the eastern and southern sides of the bawn area. The rest of the east curtain wall was clearly built bit by bit over the fill of the earlier ditch and the infilled sunken structures. With such poor foundations, it is not surprising that the wall needed constant repairs. Contrary to expectations, there was no tower at the south-eastern corner. The wall angled westwards and, unless there was a higher-level turret or bartizan, this must have been the weakest point in terms of defence.

As a royal castle with a garrison, King John's was in the charge of constables. There was no keep, the towers being used for accommodation. Its primary function from the later thirteenth century seems from the historical sources to have been for the retention of hostages or prisoners and by 1297, with the addition of the west wall, an underground chamber was built presumably for this purpose. The construction of the castle to the north of the Hiberno-Norse town left undefended a tract of land, St Nicholas's parish. This was eventually walled on the western side. From the way that this wall abuts the south-west tower of the castle, it was evidently built later.

The eastern side of the Englishtown was dominated by the religious orders. To the north of St Peter's the Dominicans founded a priory dedicated to St Saviour in 1227, while to the south a Franciscan friary was founded in 1267. The combined priory and hospital of St Mary, St Edward King and Martyr, and the Holy Cross was established by the Fratres Cruciferi in the early thirteenth century. This was located to the south-east of the town near Baal's Bridge. All of these would have been surrounded by their own walls. With the exception of St Francis's Friary, they were incorporated into the town wall precinct following the suppression of the monasteries. From recent investigations carried out north of St Saviour's, it seems that the medieval wall of the priory terminated there and that a later wall of poor construction was added around the northern end of the town. On a map of 1752 by Philip Eyres this wall is described as 'extremely bad, and very narrow in many places'.

The walls, gates and towers of the Englishtown surrounded an area of 29½ acres. Within this were all the factors necessary for the survival of an urban community. Trading both with the rural hinterland and abroad took place. It was a thriving port: the harbour was located at the south-western corner of the town. Markets were held, although the location of the market-place is unknown. The linear street pattern was focused on the High Street with long narrow properties fronting it. Access to the rear of these was by lanes at right-angles to the High Street. There were three parish churches, the cathedral and four religious houses.

Across the Abbey River from the Englishtown developed the Irishtown, so called because of its occupation by native Irish who had presumably been dispossessed of their property. This suburb was walled in the period from 1310 to 1495, enclosing an area of 27½ acres. Excavations here have shown that medieval property boundaries survived up to the recent past. Although the excavations were limited to the rear of these properties, owing to the presence of eighteenth- or nineteenth-century cellars along the frontages, there is evidence that this area was primarily occupied by craftworkers involved in the manufacture of leather, metal and bone artefacts. There were some late medieval stone houses, but the majority were of clay and wattle or cage-work, a situation that continued up to the time of the Civil Survey. The street pattern of the Irishtown was Y-shaped. A main street extended in length from Baal's Bridge to John's Gate, with Mungret Street leading off it to the south-west. There was a series of lanes giving access to the backs of the long narrow properties fronting the main street, lanes that survived up to the recent development of the area. There were no administrative buildings in the Irishtown and only two parish churches: St John's at the southern end and St Michael's outside the walls, to the west of the Water Gate.

The town walls of the Irishtown were built over a period of nearly 200 years. The murage grants imply that the earliest section was to the north, near Baal's Bridge. In a two-phase excavation of the north-western corner at Charlotte's Quay a portion of the wall and the West Water Gate were exposed, together with an inner water gate and a tower-house. The West Water Gate consisted of an arched opening flanked by two D-shaped towers. Access from the main street was by a cobbled lane, the surface of which was worn by cart-wheel ruts. About half-way down, the inner gate consisting of a square tower spanned the lane. Abutting this on the northern side was the tower-house. The area along the river bank seems to have been reclaimed gradually by building a series of walls parallel to the bank and infilling behind them.

All of these excavations in the Irishtown provided evidence of occupation in the medieval period. It is clear from both the cartographic evidence and the Civil Survey, however, that the houses were confined to a band along these frontages and that the area between this and the walls was open space, used as gardens or orchards. These areas became built-up only at a much later stage.

Further evidence illustrating the segregation of the two towns is reflected in the medieval pottery assemblages found on the excavated sites. Those in the Englishtown produced imported ware, of English or French origin, in greater or equal quantity to native Irish ware. On the Irishtown sites, however, the majority of the pottery was native with some imported ware, mainly from France and relatively little ware of English origin.

The political and economic circumstances of the late thirteenth and the fourteenth centuries created little need for expansion beyond the existing limits of the walls. Limerick's economic survival depended on its ability to cope with political change. The constant warring of both the Irish and the Anglo-Norman factions probably meant little to the townspeople, who remained loyal to the crown. In common with other modern cities, little remains on the ground that can be described as dating to the fifteenth and sixteenth centuries other than a layer of relatively disturbed or sterile soil, often referred to as garden soil separating the medieval and post-medieval horizons. The reason for this may lie partly in the ground disturbance caused by the reinforcing of the inside of the town wall with a clay rampart during the sieges of 1690 and 1691 in the Irishtown and probably in some places in the Englishtown.

David Wolfe in 1574 wrote a description of Limerick. In it he distinguishes clearly between the two towns: one he refers to as the city, the other as the borough of the city. Of the former he says:

> *Limerick is the mightiest and most beautiful of all the cities of Ireland. Fortified by great walls of vivid marble, the city forms an island in the fast-flowing River Shannon and is accessible only by two stone bridges ... For the most part, the houses are made of squared blocks of black marble and built in the style of towers or fortresses.*

He says that there were some 800 or 900 households in the city, all but a few of them being Catholic, implying that the Reformation had had little effect on the townspeople. The castle is described as unoccupied and in decay. The Irishtown, or the 'borough of the city', is described as 'better fortified than the city itself'.

Perhaps the best picture of Limerick in the late sixteenth century is that shown on the 1590 map. Although this is inaccurate in terms of scale, many of the details it portrays have been proved correct. During work done on the site of the present civic offices, a bridge of two arches was uncovered extending into the river towards a mill. There was a small gate in the town wall leading out to this bridge, the masonry of which was bonded to the town wall. Immediately north of the bridge was another doorway that gave access to an undercroft. This structure was originally built in the thirteenth century, but was later modified by the insertion of an arcade dividing it in two. The gate, the door and the bridge are all shown on the map, as are the differences in the house types: those on the High Street to the south of Newgate are fortified stone houses, examples of which still survive, while those off the High Street and to the north of Newgate are smaller and probably of cage-work. The monastic properties are, except for St Francis's Friary, all included in the walled area, and there is an inner wall extending along Bishop Street to the Island Gate. In the Irishtown the houses are mainly of cage-work with very few stone ones. The inner and outer water gates are shown, but the tower-house to the north is not delineated clearly, possibly because it is viewed from the back. There is no obscurity, however, about the location of the mural towers and gates in both the Englishtown and the Irishtown. Altogether the picture is one of two well-defended and prosperous towns.

Select bibliography

B. Bradshaw: 'Fr Wolfe's description of Limerick city, 1574', *North Munster Antiquarian Journal*, xvii (1975), pp. 47–53.

J. Dowd: *History of Limerick*, ed. C. O'Carroll, Dublin, 1990.

J. Hill: *The Building of Limerick*, Cork, 1991.

H. G. Leask: 'The ancient walls of Limerick', *North Munster Antiquarian Journal*, ii (1941), pp. 95–108 [map now out of date].

M. Lenihan: *Limerick: its History and Antiquities ...*, Dublin, 1866, reprinted Cork, 1991.

P. J. O'Connor: *Exploring Limerick's Past: an Historical Geography of Urban Development in County and City*, Newcastle West, 1987.

M. Seoighe: *Portrait of Limerick*, London, 1982.

S. Spellissy and J. O'Brien: *Limerick, the Rich Land*, Ennis,1989.

L. Walsh: *Historic Limerick: the City and its Treasures*, The Irish Heritage Series, no. 45, Dublin, 1984.

T. J. Westropp, R. A. S. Macalister and G. U. MacNamara: *The Antiquities of Limerick and its Neighbourhood*, Dublin, 1916.

THREE TOWNS: LIMERICK SINCE 1691

Eamon O'Flaherty

LIMERICK is a modern city built around and on top of a medieval core. The medieval city, however obscured by centuries of change, still survives in buildings, place-names and street patterns that have endured for at least 800 years in some places. But the modern city, as it developed after the treaty of 1691, added to the medieval fabric in ways that are particularly striking to the urban historian. The two towns of medieval Limerick became three in the course of the eighteenth and early nineteenth centuries. The Englishtown and the Irishtown acquired a rational extension in the ordered geometry of Georgian town planning called the Newtown, or Newtown Pery. Yet despite the spectacular growth and success of the Newtown, the medieval and the more recent parts of the city preserved their distinctive personalities to an unusual degree. The contrast between the narrow winding streets of the medieval city and the regular, planned grid of the eighteenth-century Newtown is a testimony to the ambitious scale of urban change in Limerick in the modern period. Few cities of Limerick's compact size offer such a comparable sense of the spatial unfolding of the different stages of urban development since the end of the seventeenth century. Fewer still offer a chance to see medieval and modern elements co-existing as they do in the three towns that compose the historic centre of Limerick.

By August 1691 Limerick had experienced two years of siege warfare. The city had sustained considerable damage by the action of the Williamite batteries on the heights of Sing-

Limerick harbour from the south-west c. 1827.

land, south-east of St John's Gate. The area around the gate suffered most, particularly from the concentrated fire that produced the ill-fated breach in the walls near the citadel. The Latin inscription commemorating the rebuilding of St John's churchyard wall is evidence both of the damage caused by war and of the determination to rebuild. Even more severe was the clearing of suburban housing undertaken as part of the work of fortification. Garryowen, or Crotagh, was more affected than Thomondgate in this process, because it lay in the front line of the city's defences. The city's external appearance changed slowly and gradually after 1691, however, since much of the work of rebuilding involved filling the gaps made by the siege rather than extensively changing the city's streets and buildings. Most dramatic, after the sieges, were the effects in February 1693 of the explosion of hundreds of barrels of gunpowder stored in one of the two towers that guarded the quay

Map by W. E. Corbett of Limerick in 1865, detail showing the Georgian Newtown.

where the potato market now stands, demolishing the tower, breaking most of the windows in the city and taking the roofs off many of the houses. Less dramatic, but more important, was the tendency to replace stone with brick in the rebuilding of houses in the principal streets. The Dutch gables of these houses reflected the influence of new fashions in domestic architecture in Ireland and Britain in the decades after the arrival of William of Orange.

The advent of brick did not, however, banish the local limestone from the streets of Limerick. The polished marble, or limestone, described by Father Wolfe in the sixteenth century continued to be favoured, particularly for important public buildings, throughout the eighteenth century. Limerick's historians have tended to paint a very gloomy picture of the city in the sixty years between the treaty and the beginning of Edmund Sexton Pery's urban renaissance. Yet these sixty years also saw a considerable amount of development that changed its appearance, particularly that of the Englishtown. Most of the public buildings of Limerick were rebuilt in classical style between 1690 and 1750, and most of them were located in an administrative district centred on Mary Street and Quay Lane, the modern Bridge Street. The mayoralty house, city and county court houses, the prison, bridewell, poor-house and Tholsel were all built or rebuilt in this period. The exchange on Nicholas Street, dating from 1673, was rebuilt several times during the eighteenth century. Nowadays only the façade of the exchange and the Gerald Griffin schools – formerly the city court house – survive from this period.

Although the area near St Mary's Cathedral housed the main administrative and public buildings, the early eighteenth-century city was densely crowded. All the traffic of the port was still concentrated in the small medieval long dock, now occupied by the potato market. The old site of the Franciscan friary at St Francis's Abbey, behind the present Sir

Harry's Mall on the island, was a flourishing industrial district in the eighteenth century. By this period many of the principal markets in the city were centred on the Irishtown, around St John's Gate. The gardens that had occupied a considerable part of the walled area, especially in the Irishtown, in previous centuries had largely been replaced by buildings by 1750. The city had certainly reached the limits of expansion possible within the old walls by the mid-eighteenth century. A combination of economic growth and organised development by Limerick merchants and landowners transformed the city over a period of seventy years after 1750.

Much of the spectacular urban development that transformed Limerick after 1750 is associated with Edmund Sexton Pery. Pery was the descendant of Edmund Sexton, who had been granted the Franciscan friary at the dissolution of the monasteries under Henry VIII. This gave him a substantial estate within the city, but it also gave him possession of the Prior's Land, a large tract running south of the city along the river on which the Georgian Newtown was built. Between 1751 and 1756 Pery developed a square of stone-built houses just inside St John's Gate, thereby initiating a dramatic period of development in Limerick. Though built inside the Irishtown walls, the houses at John's Square represented a new set of architectural values. In 1760 the walls were demolished south of the square to allow rear access, and a new street, later called Cornwallis Street, now Gerald Griffin Street, was laid out.

Pery was not alone in promoting expansion in this period, however, and the development of John's Square in the 1750s was followed very quickly by an extensive programme of building on the riverside between the two historic parts of the city. Central to the construction of the new quays around Baal's Bridge was the increase of the traffic of the port. The government's plan to extend the navigation of the Shannon resulted in grants to make the river navigable between Limerick and

Killaloe, which involved cutting a canal between the Abbey River at Baal's Bridge and the Shannon at Rhebogue. This involved building a lock and system of quays east of the bridge, which together with the Lock Mills were completed by 1765. Baal's Bridge was widened somewhat by the demolition of the houses along its east side, but communication between the Englishtown and the Pery lands to the south was ensured by the building of a new bridge with parliamentary grants in 1762. Between the two bridges regular quays were built – George's Quay and Charlotte's Quay – which were occupied by four-storey Georgian terraces. The architectural highlight of this development was the completion of Davis Ducart's Custom House in 1767.

Within just over ten years the city had broken its old boundaries and was set on a pattern of development that produced the Georgian Newtown by the 1820s. By 1787 Bank Place, Rutland Street and the triangular development of Arthur's Quay, Francis Street and Patrick Street had been built, giving the city its first recognisably Georgian district. It is significant, too, that these developments were undertaken not by Pery, but by two of the leading Catholic merchant families – the Arthurs and the Roches – the latter being also responsible for the enormous grain-store, the Granary, in Michael Street that has recently been restored. More important was the fact that by the end of the 1760s a blueprint existed for the development of Newtown Pery along a north-south rectangular grid, to be built on the Pery estate in South Prior's Land along the axis of a great central street – George's Street, now O'Connell Street.

Politics, commerce and fashion all combined to ensure the success of the rectilinear town plan mapped out by Christopher Colles for Pery's estate in 1769. Politically the Newtown's development was helped by the increasing dissatisfaction of large numbers of the prosperous citizens with the corporation, resulting in repeated efforts from the 1750s onwards to reform the corporation and, from 1808, the establishment of self-government for the Newtown through the St Michael's parish commissioners, who assumed responsibility for paving, lighting and policing the area. The main impetus for change was, however, the sustained economic growth of the period, based primarily on the provisions trade. Although the central core of the Newtown's development was formed by the Georgian terraces of the grid around George's Street, the streets between Patrick Street and the Irishtown quickly developed into a district of warehouses and markets, of which the milk market and the old linen hall at Carr Street are surviving examples. Further south, below William Street, the Georgian terraces were complemented by large stone warehouses, especially on the streets between George's Street and the river.

The initial division of the Newtown into rectangular lots was important in maintaining a sense of unity in the development. This architectural unity, which struck contemporary observers so favourably and which still defines the centre of Limerick, was achieved despite the fact that the Newtown is not the work of a single architect or landlord. Blocks were leased and built upon by individuals over a long period of time and the area did not assume its final shape until the 1820s and 1830s, when the last streets, such as Hartstonge Street, Catherine Place and The Crescent, were built. Pery Square, which was never fully realised, was laid out in the 1830s, by which time the era of Georgian building that gave us the Newtown was coming to an end. But with relatively small variations, the streets leading from the new bridge of 1762 southwards to The Crescent and Pery Square conform to the prevailing canons of eighteenth-century town planning, defining the streetscape by their adherence to fixed proportions and ordered, harmonious symmetry. They combine to form an architectural heritage of great urbanity and considerable beauty.

Cultural life in the eighteenth century centred on the coffee houses of Quay Lane, but the building of the Assembly Rooms on Charlotte's Quay in 1770 and of the Commercial Buildings in Patrick Street in 1806 initiated a migration of fashion and commerce from the historic centre. Theatres, clubs and places of recreation followed the trend. The Limerick Institution opened in 1809 in George's Street; Roche's Hanging Gardens built in 1808 and Joseph Fogerty's Theatre Royal of 1841, both in Henry Street, added to the relocation of the commercial and fashionable centre of Limerick in the Newtown. The success of the new development was clear, for the centre of gravity of the city moved inexorably southwards from the 1770s onwards as public and commercial buildings were increasingly located in the new district. After the establishment of Maunsell's Bank in Bank Place in 1789, new banks were concentrated predominantly in O'Connell Street and Glentworth Street during the nineteenth century as commercial interests abandoned the old city.

With the movement of population south, there was a corresponding pattern of church building in the newer parts of the city. The migration of the more prosperous part of the population was reflected in church building by all denominations in the late eighteenth and early nineteenth centuries. The most striking development in the pre-Victorian period, however, before the massive expansion of the Catholic Church, was the scale of building by the Church of Ireland and other Protestant churches in the city up to the 1840s. An octagonal stone church, which was never completed, was originally to have formed the centrepiece of the Newtown. St George's Church was built in 1789 as a chapel of ease for the Church of Ireland in George's Street, but later became a bank after the building of St Michael's in Pery Square in 1844. Four Presbyterian, Methodist and Quaker chapels were built in the area between 1812 and 1821, replacing earlier buildings in the Englishtown. Trinity

Chapel in Catherine Place, built in 1834, still adds dignity to the street on which it stands, though now converted into offices.

In the early nineteenth century the orderly development of the Newtown streets contrasted with the more haphazard growth of the quays downriver of the new custom house. Quay building, like house building, had been undertaken by individuals but these privately-built quays, still often identified by the names of the original builders, proved inadequate to the growing demands of the port and a series of massive improvements, funded by loans from the government, culminated in the building of a regular line of quays from Honan's Quay to O'Neill's Quay in the 1830s and, in 1853, the completion of the floating dock below Mount Kennet. The original plan of the 1820s envisaged damming the river at the site of the new Wellesley Bridge and creating a modern harbour closer to the custom-house, but this plan came to nothing, partly due to the high costs of the bridge itself. The magnetic attraction of the new port for industry is evident in the large-scale industrial buildings that were constructed around the new docks area in the nineteenth century, increasingly using steam power, the most dramatic of which were the Newtown Pery Mills at Mount Kennet, and Bannatyne's Mills across the river, operating amidst a thriving industrial quarter containing smaller mills, factories, the principal gasworks and dozens of stores and yards, all in close proximity to the docks. As much as the sedate elegance of Newtown Pery at mid-century, the bustling, hard-working docks area, which acquired its own network of residential streets, particularly around the old Windmill district, expressed the personality of the developing city by the middle of the nineteenth century.

The remarkable vigour of Limerick's expansion in the century after 1760 took place at the expense of the historic centre. The desertion of the old city by the wealthier citizens, and the movement of the port and its related industry to the south, abandoned the old city to a long period of decline and neglect. Despite its historic importance, the Englishtown suffered considerably in the nineteenth century. Although still the seat of the courts, and improved by the building of a new county court house and city gaol on Merchants' Quay, the verdict of observers from the early nineteenth century was of a run-down medieval quarter overshadowed by the modern city to the south. Old St Munchin's Church, at the north end of the Englishtown, was rebuilt in 1827, around the time that Villier's almshouses were built close by, as was St John's Church in the Irishtown in 1843. But these did little to compensate for the relocation of most public building in the newer parts of the town, a move symbolised by the migration of the town hall to Patrick Street in 1843 and the abandonment of the exchange in Nicholas Street. The nineteenth-century Irishtown was a warren of small lanes branching off from the three main streets – John Street, Mungret Street and Broad Street – occupied by small two-room cottages built in rows on either side of the lanes, and producing the highest densities of houses and people in the city. Both the older suburbs of Thomondgate and Garryowen continued to grow as historic extensions of the old city and both reflected the predominantly working-class character of the Englishtown and the Irishtown. Despite its long decline in importance, the historic centre of the city remained the home of the majority of the working population until well into the present century.

The great legacy of the Victorian period was in terms of industrial and institutional buildings rather than domestic architecture. By 1900 there were four army barracks in the city, the largest of them south of the Newtown. Between 1811 and 1825 Mulgrave Street had become an institutional district as an imposing prison, county infirmary and mental hospital were built. The 1841 workhouse in Shelbourne Road replaced the

1774 House of Industry on the North Strand, while the old centre got its share of institutional building through the erection of St John's Hospital at St John's Gate in 1785 and Barrington's Hospital on George's Quay in 1831. Perhaps the most distinctive contribution to the city's architecture was provided by the enormous increase in Catholic churches, convents and schools in the course of the nineteenth century. From small beginnings in the eighteenth century, large imposing parish churches were built in the older parts of the city, culminating in St John's Cathedral in 1859. The growth of the Newtown was registered by the building of substantial churches there by the main religious orders – Franciscans, Augustinians, Dominicans and Jesuits. On an even greater scale were the schools and convents of the new Irish religious orders like the Sisters of Mercy and the Christian Brothers. The pace of expansion continued in the later part of the century and the predominantly Catholic allegiance of the city was forcefully expressed in stone and brick, often in the classical style of the city's architecture, but increasingly in the Gothic revival that was characteristic of the century.

The arrival of the railways after 1848 confirmed the southern shift of the city centre. The railway terminus added to the industrial growth of the area in its immediate vicinity. In 1870 a large new market complex was built between Cathedral Place and Mulgrave Street, connected to the railway by a branch line across Mulgrave Street. The markets and railway district became the centre of most of the city's meat processing factories and the development of railway works and of Peter Tait's giant clothing factory in Prospect provided a south-eastern industrial centre balancing the docks area. Indeed the result was to cramp the potential expansion of the fashionable Newtown, and had consequences for the development of the residential suburbs of the late nineteenth and early twentieth centuries. The Newtown continued to expand along the line of

O'Connell Street, as Victorian suburbs developed along the military road laid out to serve the New Barracks, now Sarsfield Barracks, in 1798, but the Clare side of the river grew in importance.

Not only were the railways and docks creating an industrial quarter around the Newtown, but also improved land communications were opening the city to its hinterland in the nineteenth century. The opening of Wellesley Bridge in 1835 connected the Newtown to the Clare side of the Shannon. The North Strand was already developing by the early nineteenth century, and the North Circular Road and Ennis Road had been laid out by 1840. The Ennis Road, like O'Connell Avenue on the south side, became an axis of Victorian suburban building, initially in the form of large villas like Shelbourne House and Rose Hill, but near the end of the century there was a trend towards building red-brick terraces along the Ennis Road similar to those on O'Connell Avenue. Park Bridge and Athlunkard Bridge also opened up communication with the northeastern hinterland. Limerick, which for so many centuries had been a fortified settlement, shielded by the river as much as by its gates and walls, had begun to expand to occupy the surrounding countryside. Kate O'Brien's fictional Limerick merchant family, the Considines, moved from an old house in the Englishtown to a high Georgian house in Newtown Pery and finally to a large villa on the Clare side of the Shannon as they grew rich. Of course the wealth of these families was based on the docks and factories of the nineteenth-century city, just as their cultural world was shaped by the great educational and religious institutions that characterised Victorian Limerick. Despite the physical and industrial expansion of the nineteenth century, Victorian Limerick did not repeat the growth pattern of the previous century. The population of the city declined gradually in the forty years after the Famine and began a modest recovery after 1891. By 1951 the city's population had recovered to the level recorded a century before, indicating the relative stagnation of southern Irish urban development in the post-Famine period.

Twentieth-century Limerick has grown out along the axes of development provided by the network of roads and bridges of the nineteenth century. The main suburbs of the present-day city were already taking shape by 1900. Since then the greatest change has taken place in the residential pattern of the population. The densely crowded working-class areas of the medieval city have largely been emptied by public housing projects undertaken since independence, and there has been a corresponding shift to the suburbs. There has also been an enormous change in the industrial face of Limerick with the decline of the port and of traditional city-centre industries. Nowadays the entire legacy of Victorian institutional building is being adapted to changes of use. During the past decade there has been an impressive commitment to urban renewal, which has resulted in the rebuilding of large areas of the historic centre that had been allowed to become derelict. This has improved both medieval and Georgian parts of the city. The civic offices at Merchants' Quay and the rebuilding of Arthur's Quay have shown that modern buildings can be introduced into an old site without destroying its historic character. Rarely, however, has there been such a high level of awareness of the cultural wealth of the city's urban heritage, a recognition that change and conservation are both integral parts of the process of urban renewal.

Select bibliography
J. Begley: *The Diocese of Limerick*, 3 vols, Dublin, 1906–22.
J. Ferrar: *History of Limerick ... from the Earliest Records to 1787*, Limerick, 1787.

D. Fitzgerald: 'Georgian Limerick', *Irish Georgian Society Bulletin*, iii, no. 4 (1960), pp. 33–46.

P. Fitzgerald and J. J. McGregor: *History, Topography and Antiquities of the County and City of Limerick*, 2 vols, Dublin, 1826–7.

J. Hill: *The Building of Limerick*, Cork, 1991.

J. Kemmy: 'Limerick limestone', in M. Ó hEochaidh (ed.), *Modhscoil Luimnigh 1855–1986*, Limerick, 1986.

M. Lenihan: *Limerick: its History and Antiquities ...*, Dublin, 1866, reprinted Cork, 1991.

C. M. Murphy: 'Building and related activities in Limerick 1859–99', *North Munster Antiquarian Journal*, xix (1977), pp. 51–63.

C. M. Murphy: 'Limerick Navigation Co. 1697–1836', *North Munster Antiquarian Journal*, xxii (1980), pp. 43–61.

P. J. O'Connor: *Exploring Limerick's Past: an Historical Geography of Urban Development in County and City*, Newcastle West, 1987.

'LIKE A LITTLE CASTLE': WATERFORD IN THE MIDDLE AGES

Terry Barry

THERE is in the possession of Waterford Corporation a unique charter roll of late fourteenth-century date. It is made up of a large number of rectangular pieces of vellum (made from the skin of calves) sewn together to make a long, narrow roll, and contains copies of a series of charters and other documents mostly relating to the bitter trade dispute that caused friction between Waterford and its near neighbour New Ross throughout most of the period from the thirteenth to the sixteenth centuries. What is even more remarkable about this roll is the sixteen painted illustrations along its left-hand side of English kings and other notable people of the time. At the top of the roll in its centre is a faded painting of the king receiving the homage of the mayor and bailiffs of the city of Waterford. Below it is a representation of the city as seen from across the River Suir, a truly remarkable scene since it is probably the earliest surviving illustration of an Irish medieval city that has survived down to the modern period. It is a fairly stylised view of a gleamingly white medieval city, much as is found in the illustrations in the later and more famous French book of hours known as the *Très Riches Heures du Duc de Berri*. Nevertheless it does portray the basic elements of Waterford's power and prosperity within the lordship of medieval Ireland: its incomparable stone walls and towers (including Reginald's Tower) within which can be seen the Franciscan friary and the

Artist's impression by Seán Durack of Waterford c. 1170.

cathedral, and at least three galleys of its significant shipping fleet that traded with much of Europe. It is on the walls, principal buildings and trade that I wish to concentrate in this short examination of medieval Waterford.

But before I write in more detail about these city walls, some comment is necessary about the name Waterford itself, especially since it is derived directly from Old Norse. This Old Norse word *Vedrarfjordr* can be traced back in the sources to as early as the late ninth or early tenth century, and has variously been interpreted by linguistic experts as meaning 'fjord of the rams' (an indication, perhaps, of one of the main exports through the port in Viking times) or, rather more prosaically, 'windy fjord'. This latter meaning probably refers to Waterford as being a port that gave safe haven to Viking ships sheltering from a storm-tossed Irish Sea in this inlet, or 'fjord' to the Scandinavians, of the Suir. Given the strategic and trading importance of the three main rivers – Barrow, Nore and Suir – in this

Charter roll showing Waterford c. 1370.

part of Ireland, it is scarcely surprising that the Vikings set up
a defended *longphort* here in about 914, which developed into
a significant urban area during the tenth century. Most scholars would now agree that this earliest fortification was located

in the vicinity of Reginald's Tower, and developed along the ridge of high ground where the principal thoroughfares of High Street and Peter Street were eventually established.

Commentators throughout the centuries have written extensively about the impressive nature of the defensive walls and towers of Waterford. For instance, in 1375 the walls were described as being 'like a little castle'. The large-scale archaeological excavations of over 20 per cent of the walled area that have taken place recently in the centre of the Hiberno-Norse town, around Arundel Square and Peter Street, have revealed that the earliest perimeter defences were made up of a wide ditch and substantial bank, probably surmounted by a wooden breastwork with a walkway behind it. This has been scientifically dated to the end of the eleventh century by counting the tree rings of several oak timber samples from both the ditch and the bank. These earthen ramparts are later than those of Dublin, but earlier than the comparable system excavated in Limerick. They survived for up to half a century before they were replaced by the construction of a stone wall that has been dated archaeologically to the second quarter of the twelfth century, just before the Anglo-Normans arrived in Ireland.

These stone walls are mentioned in one of the most famous passages in the *Expugnatio Hibernica* ('The Conquest of Ireland') by Gerald of Wales, in which he describes the capture of the walled city of Waterford by Raymond le Gros and his Anglo-Norman army in 1170. After his forces were twice repulsed by the defenders, Le Gros noticed 'a small building which hung down from the town wall on the outside by a beam'. He had this beam cut down, which caused the building to collapse on to the city wall, thus creating a sizeable breach through which the Anglo-Normans were able to pass and take the city. This account gives us a fascinating insight into the overcrowding that was affecting the city, in that buildings were being allowed to encroach upon its perimeter defences, as also happened in Dublin later on in the Middle Ages. A little further on in this account there is mention of Reginald's Tower in which the two Sitrics, leaders of the Norse within the city, were hiding. This confirms that this, the most famous of Waterford's towers, located at the north-eastern corner of the city where it meets the Suir, was already in existence before the Anglo-Norman period. The tower, which we can still see today, is probably a rebuilding of this original tower in the late twelfth century, and corporation workmen are currently stripping away the later plaster from its interior to reveal its complex building history. At least one other tower, Turgesius's Tower, probably dates to the Hiberno-Norse era, although it does not survive. This tower is thought to have been located near to the present-day Allied Irish Bank branch on Barronstrand, where it meets the quayside along the Suir.

After the Anglo-Normans captured the city they refortified the walls and added towers and gates to the circuit. There was an expansion westwards of the city in the early thirteenth century, caused by the rapid growth in population and the expulsion of the Ostmen, the descendants of the Viking invaders. By the end of the Middle Ages the size of the walled area had virtually doubled, with some fifteen gates and twenty-three mural towers along the circuit. Most of these were concentrated along the south-western and western sides of the city, for the Suir provided a natural barrier to the north. They were also less frequent to the east and south-east, where a large marshy area and the John's River provided additional protection. Fifteenth-century documents refer to the 'king's fosse', which divided the older walled city from the suburbs and enhanced the overall defensive capability of the walls. Traces of it were located during the recent archaeological excavations. As early as 1224 we learn of the existence of gates such as Colbeck, St Martin's and Arundel, all of which have long since disappeared. In the early 1980s, however, St Martin's Gate was archaeologically excavated after it was discovered on a site cleared for the construction of a new school. The two small drum-shaped towers there are comparable to other thirteenth-century gate towers such as the well-known St Lawrence's Gate in Drogheda.

This formidable circuit, testifying to the economic wealth of the city, was largely paid for out of the murage grant conceded by the crown to the citizens from as early as 1207. These grants allowed the burgesses of Waterford to levy a tax on a large variety of commodities that included wine, hides, cloth and iron passing through the port in order to raise the necessary funds to keep their walls maintained. Indeed Waterford has the best surviving series of medieval murage charters in Ireland. And, what is even more striking, the inhabitants seem to have used some of this money on their walls, unlike many other medieval townspeople.

Nevertheless maintaining these extensive walls, gates and towers caused continual problems for the mayor and burgesses right into the late Middle Ages. For instance, in 1430 Waterford was granted £30 a year to be spent 'on the repair and defence of the town', since 'the ditches, walls, towers, gates and portcullises are so old and ruinous in many places as to be all but fallen to the ground'. They were obviously kept in good repair in this difficult century, because in 1495 the city was able to withstand a siege that allowed its garrison to take part in the defeat of the army of Perkin Warbeck, the pretender to the English throne.

Within these walls, as can be seen in the charter roll painting, there were impressive stone structures such as the cathedral, which survived until 1770. Traces of the early thirteenth-century structure can still be seen in the crypt of the Protestant cathedral that now occupies its site. But it must be remembered that most of the houses and other buildings within the Viking and later medieval city were either of wattle or wooden-framed construction, as has been confirmed by the recent archaeological excavations in the Peter Street area. In a crowded medieval city such as Waterford the risk from fire was very real, as Friar John Clyn of Kilkenny reminds us in his *Annals* that in 1252 there was a drought followed by a fire in Waterford, followed by another fire in 1280. The danger from fire was recognised by the city authorities as early as 1300, when the borough customs demanded that anyone who set a street on fire was to be cast into the flames as a punishment! Somewhat later in the same century, in 1388–9, a law was enacted to get rid of all shops and other tenements that were roofed with straw or herbage. In a major conflagration only the churches and principal buildings in stone would have survived, along with the cellars and undercrofts of the more prosperous inhabitants.

As well as the cathedral Waterford had seven parish churches and several religious houses, such as those of the Benedictines, Dominicans, Augustinians, and the Franciscans whose friary is probably portrayed on the charter roll. There were other minor religious houses and hospitals founded from the twelfth century onwards. For instance, the Hospitallers of St John were granted a site in the Arundel Square area of the city in 1212. An impressive stone and post-hole structure with surviving floorboards dating to the thirteenth century was found during the recent archaeological excavations in this locality, and this could have been part of the hospital. These excavations also uncovered one of the two pre-Norman parish churches of the city, St Peter's, and its cemetery. Like many other buildings in the city it enters the historical record only in the later medieval period, but its earliest levels have been dated archaeologically to the twelfth century. It was found to have an apse, which is a unique survival in any medieval parish church in Ireland, although there are apses in the central chapels of the transepts of the twelfth-century Cistercian monastery at Mellifont in County Louth. The fact that the church is dedicated to St Peter could also represent the triumph of the Roman reform movement in Ireland after the council of Cashel (1101). Perhaps the founder had returned recently from a pilgrimage to Rome and wished therefore to dedicate his church to the first pope.

Curiously enough for such an important royal city, there is today no physical evidence for the construction of a large castle similar to those built in other cities such as Dublin or Limerick. The very strength of its walls may have rendered unnecessary the strategic requirement for such a castle, although some fifteenth-century documents refer to an old wall that was part of King John's castle. But we do know that there was a mint in the city at the end of the thirteenth century, and a guild-hall at the start of that century.

Now let us turn finally to the galleys that are portrayed in this 1370 illustration of the city. As well as being a major port, Waterford seems to have supplied many ships to the crown for prosecuting war both in Ireland and beyond, and for carrying the goods that were the life-blood of the port's international trade. Obviously during its Hiberno-Norse phase there must have been a large fleet based in the city. This is confirmed by the historical record at the end of the eleventh century when the would-be king of Gwynedd, Gruffydd ap Cynan, was provided with a Waterford fleet by Diarmait Ua Briain, the king of Munster, to aid him in his attempt to secure the kingship of that part of Wales. It is scarcely surprising, then, that this shipbuilding tradition survived into the thirteenth century, when many royal mandates were issued for the construction of warships. In 1256 twenty-three ships with 600 horses on board were sent from Waterford to Milford Haven to help put down the rebellion of Llywelyn ap Gruffydd in Wales. This dependence on Waterford for military ships continued into the following century, as can be seen in the instructions of 1311 requesting the city to send three ships 'fully armed and provisioned for seven weeks' to Larne in County Antrim to join the large royal fleet being assembled there to sail against the forces of Robert Bruce in the Western Isles of Scotland. Eventually the crown was to triumph with the death of Edward Bruce at the battle of Faughart, County Louth, in 1318. Nevertheless the 'invasion years' from 1315 to 1318 when Scottish armies were laying waste much of Ireland proved to be a severe shock to the security of the English lordship here, with its full resources, including those of its principal towns such as Waterford, being utilised to meet this threat.

It is possible that the three galleys portrayed at the top of the charter roll were similar to the *Margarete* which we know was owned by William Fithian, one of the bailiffs of the city at the beginning of the fourteenth century. Or it may have been the *Marie* which traded between La Rochelle and Scotland at the end of the same century, and which was constructed in Waterford. It is interesting to speculate that one of the main cargoes to be carried in a ship such as this would have been wine from the Bordeaux region of France. Some idea of the full cargo of Irish exports carried by these trading vessels can be got from a surviving legal document of 1327, when merchants from Dinan in Brittany had a vessel laden in Waterford with wool, hides, salmon, cheese, cloth, silver plate and other smaller items to the value of some £600, destined for the port of Bruges in Flanders. These raw materials were among the principal goods exported from this region of Ireland in this period. The rich hinterland based around the three great rivers – Barrow, Nore and Suir – supplied these commodities to the market at Waterford. The port's importance as a wool exporter was recognised in the middle of the fourteenth century when it was made one of the four Irish ports from which wool and hides could be exported.

It is therefore instructive to examine the customs returns

on wool and wool products for Ireland at the end of the thirteenth century and the start of the fourteenth. These commodities, more than any others, were of central importance to the export trade from south-eastern Ireland in the Middle Ages. Thus it is not surprising that the two almost contiguous ports of New Ross and Waterford between them paid over half the entire custom. We cannot, of course, be sure of the extent of tax evasion in particular ports, especially since the biggest city, Dublin, paid so little tax, but the likelihood is that the two south-eastern ports did dominate this trade. The downside of this was the resulting 'trade war' that continued on and off between them from the thirteenth until the early sixteenth century. Although New Ross was smaller than Waterford, and did not benefit directly from royal favour unlike its larger rival, it was part of the powerful Marshal lordship of Leinster. It was also the largest exporter of hides, wool and woolfells in the medieval colony in this period. Indeed it was probably as a result of this dispute that the famous charter roll was compiled soon after 1370, to show how the crown was always ready to grant the necessary charters and writs to Waterford. This trade dispute often resulted in violence, as can be seen in 1266 when the burgesses of New Ross had forcibly diverted forty ships, killing two men in the process. Even as late as 1518 we learn that thirty-four leading citizens of Waterford, accompanied by 'many Spaniards, Frenchmen, Bretons and Irish', attacked New Ross and did £100 worth of damage before being bought off by the gift of a silver-gilt mace. Throughout most of this dispute the crown supported Waterford, especially since the city was strategically important when royal armies landed in Ireland, and because of its central role as a royal port supplying provisions for both its domestic and its foreign wars.

The eminent economic historian, Eleanora Carus-Wilson, writing about the port facilities of Waterford at the end of the Middle Ages, described the 'extensive quay of half a mile [where] no less than sixty ships could anchor', and this probably more than made up for the fact that its walled area was smaller than that of its main rival, New Ross. In fact it was similar in size to those of Dublin and Limerick, two other cities with a Hiberno-Norse origin, and of Southampton in southern England, with which it carried on much trade. Indeed Waterford's mercantile success in this period must owe much to its geographical position within easy sailing distance from Bristol and Chester, the two west coast English ports that specialised in trading with Ireland. It was also well situated in regard to the western half of France, which was still under English rule, and to the ports of La Rochelle and Bordeaux in particular.

Mention of these two French ports reminds us that another principal commodity that brought great profit to Waterford in the Middle Ages was wine from Gascony. Many of the beautifully glazed polychrome jugs from the Saintogne pottery kilns situated to the north of Bordeaux, which were found during the archaeological excavations in the city, were probably filled with this wine when they were exported to Ireland. This wine trade was extremely important to the economic well-being of the city because of the tax known as the prisage of wine. In 1232 we learn that two hogsheads (which were casks containing 52½ gallons) of wine, at a value of 20s. each, were to be exacted from every ship coming into Waterford to unload, one for the crown and the other for the burgesses. We can gain some insight into the tremendous profits that could be made from this trade from a reference for the year 1300, when Waterford acted as an entrepôt for the major portion of 3,000 hogsheads of wine from Bordeaux that were re-exported to the port of Skinburness to supply the army of King Edward I in Scotland. Not only were 20s. levied on each hogshead for this tax, but there was an additional murage levy of at least 12d. a ship as well, to keep the walls maintained. When it is realised that the average wage for a skilled craftsman during this period was 1½d. a week, it soon becomes apparent how much profit the burgesses of Waterford could look forward to in the boom times of the Middle Ages.

In the second half of the fourteenth century Waterford, like many other urban centres within the lordship, would have suffered economically as a result of the Great European Famine (1315–18), which coincided with the Bruce invasion, and the Black Death (1348–50). This latter event could well have carried off between 25 per cent and 50 per cent of the crowded urban population. If this was not enough of a problem to the well-being of the city, there were almost constant occurrences of 'murrains' or livestock diseases throughout the thirteenth and fourteenth centuries, which must have had an adverse effect on the city's hinterland and therefore on its export trade. Its eastern side must have been badly inundated by the floods that we know from the annals were prevalent in the middle of the fourteenth century. However, it must be stressed that, despite all the complaints of decline and decay made by the city's burgesses to the crown in the late Middle Ages, the city largely survived the political instability of the period safe and secure behind its powerful walls. This interpretation is given added weight by all the references to its trade continuing through this difficult era, especially as its now largely Gaelic-Irish hinterland benefited economically in no small measure from the uninterrupted continuance of this trade. As Art Cosgrove has so cogently stated, 'the profits of trade, like those of warfare, had an attraction that surmounted the ethnic divide'.

These, then, were some of the elements of the mercantile importance and power of Waterford, which dominated much of the south coast throughout the Middle Ages. In the next chapter Julian Walton will continue this story from the sixteenth century onwards, when Waterford was generally showered with favours by the Tudor monarchs. But, as we have seen, even in the Middle Ages it lived up to its proud late medieval motto given by King Henry VII – *Urbs intacta manet Waterfordia* (the city of Waterford remains untaken).

Select bibliography

J. Bradley and A. Halpin: 'The topographical development of Scandinavian and Anglo-Norman Waterford', in W. Nolan and T. P. Power (eds), *Waterford: History and Society*, Dublin, 1992, pp. 105–29.

J. S. Carroll: 'Some notes on Waterford maps and plans', *Decies*, xx (1982), pp. 29–38.

M. F. Hurley: 'Late Viking Age settlement in Waterford city', in W. Nolan and T. P. Power (eds), *Waterford: History and Society*, Dublin, 1992, pp. 49–72.

J. F. Lydon: 'The city of Waterford in the later Middle Ages', *Decies*, xii (1979), pp. 5–15.

E. McEneaney: 'Waterford and New Ross trade competition, *c.* 1300', *Decies*, xii (1979), pp. 16–24.

E. McEneaney: 'The government of the municipality of Waterford in the thirteenth century', *Decies*, xiii (1980), pp. 17–27.

E. McEneaney: 'Mayors and merchants in medieval Waterford', in W. Nolan and T. P. Power (eds), *Waterford: History and Society*, Dublin, 1992, pp. 147–76.

P. Power: 'The town wall of Waterford', *Journal of the Royal Society of Antiquaries of Ireland*, lxxiii (1943), pp. 118–36.

A. Thomas: *The Walled Towns of Ireland*, Dublin, 1992, i, *passim*; ii, pp. 200–10.

Waterford Corporation: *The Royal Charters of Waterford*, Waterford, 1992.

FROM *URBS INTACTA* TO CRYSTAL CITY: WATERFORD 1495–1995

Julian Walton

IN the last chapter Dr Terry Barry referred to a description of the walls of Waterford in 1375 as being 'like a little castle'. It is significant that the expression was coined by the citizens themselves, and indeed they might have said the same thing of their city two hundred years later. For throughout much of the sixteenth century Waterford remained a medieval town. Its population, largely confined by the sturdy walls and many towers, was loyal to the conveniently remote English monarchy and sturdily defiant of its immediate surroundings. In 1495 the citizens successfully resisted an eleven-day siege by land and water conducted by Perkin Warbeck, pretender to the throne of England, and his chief Irish supporter the earl of Desmond. Their determination was rewarded by a grateful Henry VII with the motto *Urbs intacta manet Waterfordia* (the city of Waterford remains untaken). A generation later, their refusal to support the rebellion of Silken Thomas and their readiness to allow the city to be used as a base for the royal armies earned them the gratitude of Henry VIII, who sent them a ceremonial sword and hat to be borne before the mayor on important occasions.

Beyond the city walls lay the hostile world of the gaelicised Anglo-Irish lords such as the Powers of Curraghmore and the Fitzgeralds of Desmond. In times of rebellion, such as the great revolts of the earls of Desmond during the reign of

Pictorial map of Waterford in 1673 (detail).

Elizabeth I, rebel armies were liable to devastate the country-side right up to the walls of the city. As late as 1518, as Dr Barry has mentioned, there was a pitched battle between the forces of Waterford and her nearest trading rival, the town of New Ross. Even on the ocean itself, Waterford men were not free from assault. In addition to the natural hazards of maritime travel, there was the constant danger of piracy, especially on the part of the aggressive and daring O'Driscolls of Baltimore. In 1538, goaded beyond endurance, the citizens retaliated by fitting out a little fleet and ransacking the territory of the O'Driscolls.

In spite of all these perils, Waterford remained throughout the sixteenth century the second city in Ireland. Her life's blood was her overseas trade, especially with Bristol and with France and Spain. English writers of the time commented frequently on the great woolly blankets in which the Irish wrapped themselves, and the copious draughts of *aqua vitae* or whiskey which they imbibed by way of refreshment. Both of these were Waterford specialities: 'As they distil the best *aqua vitae*, so they spin the choicest rug in Ireland', wrote the Dubliner Richard Stanihurst. Gifts of both were often sent by Waterford mayors to prominent courtiers by way of 'sweeteners'. One friend of Stanihurst who visited London wrapped in a Waterford rug nearly ended up as a sweetener himself, being mistaken for a bear by the hounds in the bear-garden; luckily for him, the mastiffs were muzzled.

The 'little castle' of Waterford was governed in the sixteenth century by a junta of about thirty families. Both racially and culturally they were a mixed lot, partly English and partly Irish. The Tudor monarchs rewarded their loyalty with a series of charters. These granted important trading and administrative privileges: in 1574, for example, the charter of Queen Elizabeth established a separate county of the city and liberties of Waterford, governed by its mayor and sheriffs and inde-

Prospect by Anthony Chearnley of Waterford from the north, 1746 (detail).

207

pendent of the county sheriff. These Tudor charters had also a symbolic importance, as had the sword and hat granted to the mayor by Henry VIII. Impressive documents consisting of several huge sheets of vellum, they were embellished with royal portraits, arms and emblems in glorious colour. Their purpose was to encourage a 'feel-good factor' that would bind the city even more closely to the monarchy.

And yet during the reign of Elizabeth relations between crown and corporation deteriorated dramatically. There were several reasons for this – the rampant inflation of the late Tudor period, the curtailment of trade with Spain, the devaluation of the coinage – but the breaking point was over religion. Waterford accepted the royal supremacy without demur, but the government's clumsy attempts to impose Protestantism were rejected with scorn. Younger sons of merchants, trained in continental seminaries, either pursued brilliant careers in the universities of Europe or returned to their native city imbued with the full vigour of the Counter-Reformation. The prestige achieved by Waterford clerics at this time is astonishing. One family, the Waddings, produced in a single generation five distinguished Jesuits and the illustrious Franciscan scholar, Luke Wadding.

Loyalty to the crown in politics but to the pope in religion was a concept intolerable to the government, especially after the excommunication of Queen Elizabeth by Pope Pius V in 1570. A rupture between the monarchy and the Munster towns that had remained staunchly Catholic was inevitable. It happened on the death of Elizabeth in March 1603. In Waterford the Catholic clergy took possession of the churches and celebrated high mass in the cathedral. A very angry Lord Mountjoy soon appeared before the city with an army of five thousand. Amazingly the citizens refused to admit them, citing their privileges under the charter of King John. This was taking the 'little castle' mentality to extremes, and Mountjoy retorted that if they did not open their gates immediately he would 'cut King John's charter with King James's sword, ruin their city and strew it with salt'. They submitted, and luckily Mountjoy was tolerant.

There followed twenty years of religious acrimony, declining trade and administrative chaos, culminating in the revocation of the city's charters in 1618 and the imposition of military rule. Already the city's fortifications had been strengthened in the aftermath of the Spanish Armada; now a great citadel was built at Ballybricken outside St Patrick's Gate, on the high ground to the west of the city. 'I have mounted some guns,' reported the governor, 'on a wooden platform, and they overlook the town.' So indeed they are shown to do in the illustration accompanying his report. The massive bulwarks were designed to defend the city from outside attack, but the guns pointed into the city.

Luke Gernon, second justice of Munster, neatly summarised Waterford's situation in 1620:

> Waterford is situated upon the best harbour, and in a pleasant and temperate air. The buildings are of English form and well compact. There is a fair cathedral, but her beauty is in the quay, for, the wall of the town extending for near half a mile along the water, between that and the water there is a broad quay, mainly fortified with stone and strong piles of timber, where a ship of the burden of 1,000 tons may ride at anchor. It was famous for merchandise, but her high stomach in disobeying the State deprived her of her magistrate, and now she is in the government of a soldier.

In 1626 King Charles I, in exchange for £3,000 ready money, granted the city a new and even more magnificent charter, the Great or Governing Charter according to which the city was administered down to the Municipal Reform Act of 1840. However, the Catholic oligarchy remained understandably suspicious of English intentions. In the appallingly confused period of feuding and fighting that followed the outbreak of rebellion in October 1641, Waterford was soon captured by an Irish army and thereafter supported the extreme Catholic position advocated by Rinuccini, the papal nuncio. The city's wholehearted support of the Counter-Reformation at this time earned her the sobriquet *Parva Roma* (Little Rome). When in November 1649 the parliamentary army under Cromwell arrived before the walls, so thoroughly did the citizens distrust the main royalist forces that, in a final fling of the 'little castle' mentality, they refused to admit a garrison until the last possible moment. They were lucky: the lateness of the season and a dramatic deterioration in the weather forced the enemy to abandon the siege, and Waterford thus gained the proud distinction of being the only city that Cromwell besieged and failed to capture. However, in the following summer, demoralised by blockade, plague and famine, the city surrendered to his son-in-law General Ireton.

The decade that followed marked the nadir of the city's fortunes. The corporation was dissolved and replaced by military rule. It was the intention of the parliamentary government to expel the Roman Catholic inhabitants from the cities of Ireland and replace them completely with English Protestant colonists. In practice, however, this proved impossible to enforce, other than at the top of the social scale. The old oligarchy of Walshes, Sherlocks, Wyses and Dobbyns lost their power for ever – apart from the brief interlude of the Jacobite restoration in 1688–90 – and many of their younger and more enterprising members went to seek their fortunes amid the commerce of France and Spain. When a new Catholic merchant class began to reach towards political power in the early nineteenth century, its members were self-made men rather than survivors of the old régime.

It was, therefore, an exclusively Protestant oligarchy – Alcocks, Barkers, Newports and so on – that controlled Waterford's affairs from the restoration of Charles II in 1660 until the

Municipal Reform Act of 1840. A pictorial map compiled in 1673 shows us the city they ruled, still largely confined within its medieval walls. A valuation carried out in 1663–4 shows that many of the buildings consisted of old-fashioned 'cage-work' or half-timbered houses, and the rentals of the dean and chapter compiled at the same period indicate that many of these were in a ruinous condition. The eighteenth century, however, was to see the transformation of Waterford from a virtually medieval town into a fine Georgian city. The century began with the demolition of the fortifications along the waterfront and the creation of 'the noblest quay in Europe', which by the end of the century extended for about a mile and had been paved throughout its length. A generation later, in 1736, the corporation commissioned the Flemish painter William van der Hagen to create a magnificent panoramic view of their city taken from the high ground on the northern side of the river. Ten years later a similar panorama was published in Smith's history of Waterford, and in 1764 the changes in the rapidly expanding city were mapped by William Richards and Bernard Scalé. These illustrations show the new line of merchants' residences and warehouses along the quay; the arcaded exchange (on the site of the present GPO), built in 1715; and the westward expansion of the city along King Street (now O'Connell Street), behind which the high ground at Ballybricken was still dominated by the Jacobean citadel. The finest example of Georgian development in this part of the city is the great house built in 1785 for the merchant William Morris, with its splendid façade, door-case, stucco-work and oval cantilever staircase. It is now the headquarters of the Harbour Commissioners and the Chamber of Commerce.

Eastwards, too, the city was beginning to expand. The marshy ground outside the medieval wall was drained to form The Mall, on which was built the magnificent palace of the Church of Ireland bishop, begun in 1741 by Richard Castle and

211

completed by a local architect named John Roberts. The 1780s witnessed the erection next to the palace – again by John Roberts – of new Assembly Rooms, which in 1813 became the City Hall and now houses also that fine Victorian survival beloved of Waterfordians, the Theatre Royal. On the other side of The Mall a terrace of residential houses was constructed for some of the city's leading merchant families, notably the Penroses (the site is now occupied mostly by the Tower Hotel). During the nineteenth century the suburb of Newtown developed downriver of The Mall as the city's main residential area; here too was built in 1849 the city's fine classical court house, the work of J. B. Keane and a local builder named Terence O'Reilly.

Abstracts of the destroyed religious census of 1766 suggest that in the mid-eighteenth century between a quarter and a third of the city's population belonged to the Established Church. Its members had three places of worship. The parish churches of St Patrick's and St Olave's were erected in the second quarter of the eighteenth century on medieval sites; the former, now shared by the Presbyterians and Methodists, survives virtually unchanged; the latter was converted to a community hall in the 1960s, its magnificent furnishings destroyed or scattered. However, the church that dominates the panoramic views of Van der Hagen and Smith is the medieval cathedral, built at the highest point of the Viking town and surmounted by a tall fifteenth-century battlemented tower. Unfortunately its crumbling Gothic gloom no longer impressed the ambitious and forward-looking Protestant oligarchy. In the 1770s it was demolished and John Roberts, whose reputation had been established by completing the palace, erected in its place what is perhaps the finest classical cathedral in Ireland.

Throughout the eighteenth century the operation of the penal laws prevented the Catholic majority from participating in the city's administration. Catholics did, however, play an increasingly important role in Waterford's commercial life, and mutual self-interest ensured that the city was comparatively free of religious bigotry. There were several mass-houses, one of which, St Patrick's Church, has survived with little change to the present day. The architectural historian Dr Mark Girouard has described it as a building of few architectural pretensions but of immense charm, vividly evocative of the period in which it was built. An even more remarkable building is the Roman Catholic cathedral, founded in 1793 at the very end of the penal era and an extraordinary testimony to the wealth and self-confidence of Waterford's Catholic community at the time. It was the last work of the ubiquitous John Roberts, who thus, in Mark Girouard's memorable words,

achieved the remarkable feat not only of designing two cathedrals in one town but of giving the two buildings an absolutely different character, each suited to its own religion. The Protestant cathedral is cool and northern, redolent of lawn sleeves and the communion service; the Catholic cathedral, with its forest of huge Corinthian columns, is warm, luscious and Mediterranean.

The same year, 1793, also saw the belated erection of the first bridge crossing the Suir to link Waterford with County Kilkenny. The work of Boston engineer Lemuel Cox, it served the city faithfully for over a century, though its tolls were bitterly resented. Known affectionately to Waterfordians as Timbertoes, it had become rickety by the early twentieth century and was replaced in 1913 by a ferro-concrete structure. This in turn was replaced in 1984 by the present Rice Bridge.

The prosperity of which Waterford's Georgian buildings provide abundant evidence depended chiefly on its overseas trade, not only with England and the European mainland as in previous centuries but increasingly with North America. In particular the Georgian period saw the dramatic expansion of the Newfoundland trade. For some years, west country merchants had made Waterford their last port of call before crossing the Atlantic to exploit the vast banks of cod off the Newfoundland coast; now they were being emulated by local merchants. Each year fleets would set off for *Talamh an Eisc* – the Fishing Ground – not only to catch the fish but to supply the participants with food, clothing and other necessities. This in turn led to the involvement of the city's resources in creating the requisite service industries for the fishing fleets and the shore community. There was also a huge migratory labour force – upwards of five thousand workers left from Waterford and its hinterland each year, and while many returned others remained in Newfoundland, where their descendants still retain their accents of south-eastern Ireland.

This was also the period of the great Waterford glass industry, founded in 1783 by the Quaker family of Penrose and continued by the Gatchells. In its heyday it employed 60–70 skilled workmen and produced about 50 tons of cut glass annually. It was never a big operation, but its products were of superb quality and George Gatchell's enthusiasm for exhibiting them ensured its worldwide reputation. Alas, lack of capital and a crushing excise duty on Irish glass brought about the closure of the factory in 1851.

It was not only the glass industry that suffered at this time. The recession that followed the end of the Napoleonic Wars caused the virtual collapse of the provisions trade, a decline in population from nearly 40,000 to 28,000, and emigration to North America at the rate of 2,000 a year. Moreover, behind the impressive Georgian façade was a warren of back streets and lanes where poverty was rampant. A series of reports compiled in 1831 in expectation of a cholera epidemic reveals a picture of overcrowding, deprivation and filth. It was far beyond the corporation's resources to obliterate the squalor; the most that could be done was to provide clean straw for bedding and to set up soup-kitchens in times of crisis.

The advent of steam power in the early nineteenth century brought back a measure of prosperity. One industry to benefit dramatically was shipbuilding. By the middle of the century there were several shipyards on the banks of the Suir, the most notable being the Neptune Works. Built by the Quaker family of Malcomson, the Neptune was designed to service the ships travelling to their mighty cotton mill at Portlaw, but it soon developed a life of its own. During its thirty-year existence, from 1847 to 1877, over forty steamships were built at the yard. These included the first steamer to trade regularly between London and St Petersburg, the first steam ice-breaker, and the first steamer to bring live cattle from America to Liverpool.

Waterford was also a major beneficiary of the railway era. By 1914 there were no fewer than six lines into and out of the city. They ran westwards to Limerick and Sligo, northwards to Kilkenny and Dublin, north-eastwards to New Ross and Dublin, eastwards (via the Barrow Bridge, which until 1982 was the longest bridge in Ireland) to Rosslare Harbour, southwards to Tramore, and south-westwards (via a second Suir crossing, the Red Iron Bridge) to Dungarvan and Cork. This railway network in turn generated further industry: the building suppliers Graves & Sons, for instance, moved their headquarters from New Ross to Waterford in order to avail themselves of the improved transport facilities. Another example of the use made by local enterprise in harnessing Victorian technology and communications is the Queen's Bacon Factory. Opened in 1864 at new premises in Ballybricken, within a few years it had 150 men and women in constant employment and was processing no fewer than two thousand carcasses a week, mainly for export to the London market.

It was not only factories that dominated the Waterford landscape a hundred years ago. The expansion of commerce led to the erection of some fine institutional buildings in the city centre, notably the GPO on the Quay and the branch offices of the leading banks. The perimeter was the usual site for the great charitable and educational buildings. The Irish Christian Brothers were founded in Waterford by Edmund Rice in 1802. The Sisters of Charity established themselves in the city as early as 1798, and in the same year the Quakers founded Newtown School. The Ursuline, Presentation, Mercy, St John of God orders and Little Sisters of the Poor all had bases in Waterford by the end of the century. In 1892 the De la Salle order erected a massive building in Newtown as their teacher training college; it is now the city's largest secondary school. An impressive Roman Catholic seminary was erected to the south-east on John's Hill in 1868, but this area is mainly dominated by hospitals: St Patrick's (the former workhouse), St Otteran's (the former lunatic asylum) and the now closed Infirmary (formerly the Leper Hospital).

The early decades of the independent Irish State were uneasy ones for Waterford, but since the end of the Second World War the city has made another of its great leaps forward. There have been new housing estates; new factories on an industrial estate established to the west of the city; and an extension of the municipal boundary in 1980 brought the area administered by the corporation up to about 10,000 acres, within which resides a population of some 40,000. Above all, the Waterford crystal industry has been resurrected, phoenix-like, thanks to the technical skill of Czech refugees and the vision of local industrialists. So successful has it become that for many people outside the area, and particularly in North America, 'Waterford' is no longer a place but a product.

Inevitably progress has been achieved at a price. For some of the city's Georgian buildings it is already too late; others have been spoiled by insensitive development; a few are currently in danger of destruction by developers or vandals or both. But at least there is a greater awareness today that we are the product of our past, and that by studying and conserving that past we are the better able to understand the present and to safeguard the future. This year, 1995, is the 500th since the city's dramatic gesture of independence by successfully resisting Perkin Warbeck. It is also the 800th since the earliest reference to a municipal government of Waterford. May the remembrance of these events help its citizens to value what they have inherited from their illustrious past!

Select bibliography

C. Byrne: 'The Waterford colony in Newfoundland, 1700–1850', in W. Nolan and T. P. Power (eds), *Waterford: History and Society*, Dublin, 1992, pp. 351–72.

D. Cowman: 'Trade and society in Waterford city, 1800–1840', in W. Nolan and T. P. Power (eds), *Waterford: History and Society*, Dublin, 1992, pp. 427–58.

E. Downey: *The Story of Waterford from the Foundation of the City to the Middle of the Eighteenth Century*, Waterford, 1914.

P. Egan: *History, Guide and Directory of County and City of Waterford*, Kilkenny [1894].

M. Girouard: 'The noblest quay in Europe', in *Town and Country*, New Haven and London, 1992, pp. 149 68.

W. Irish: 'Shipbuilding in Waterford', *Decies*, no. 46 (1992), pp. 40–60.

R. Lahert: 'Some charitable institutions of old Waterford', *Decies*, nos 28 (1985), pp. 43–53; 29 (1985), pp. 24–31.

K. Milne: 'The corporation of Waterford in the eighteenth century', in W. Nolan and T. P. Power (eds), *Waterford: History and Society*, Dublin, 1992, pp. 331–50.

E. O'Connor: *A Labour History of Waterford*, Waterford, 1989.

S. Pender (ed.): *Council Books of the Corporation of Waterford 1662–1700*, Dublin, 1964.

List of Contributors

Dr Terry Barry	Department of Medieval History, Trinity College, Dublin
Mr John Bradley	Department of Archaeology, University College, Dublin
Dr Howard B. Clarke	Department of Medieval History, University College, Dublin
Dr Maura Cronin	Department of History, Mary Immaculate College, Limerick
Prof. Louis Cullen	Department of Modern History, Trinity College, Dublin
Dr Raymond Gillespie	Department of Modern History, St Patrick's College, Maynooth
Mr Maurice F. Hurley	Cork Corporation, City Hall, Cork
Prof. Gearóid Mac Niocaill	Department of History, University College, Galway
Dr Eamon O'Flaherty	Department of Modern History, University College, Dublin
Ms Celie O'Rahilly	Limerick Corporation, City Hall, Limerick
Prof. Gearóid Ó Tuathaigh	Department of History, University College, Galway

Dr Jacinta Prunty   Department of Geography, University College, Dublin

Dr Stephen Royle   School of Geosciences, Queen's University, Belfast

Dr Avril Thomas   Department of Environmental Studies, University of Ulster, Coleraine

Mr Julian Walton   Waterford

IRISH COUNTRY TOWNS

Edited by
Anngret Simms and J. H. Andrews

Country towns are an important aspect of Irish identity, blending place and time in a unique fashion. Their stories reflect the formative periods of town foundation in Ireland: from Gaelic monastic sites to Anglo-Norman colonial settlements to early modern plantation towns.

The story of each town is here given added interest by a town plan and an evocative black-and-white illustration, usually nineteenth-century. A map gives an overview of all the towns featured in the book and classifies them according to their mode of origin.

The collective history of these Irish towns reflects the complexity of Irish civilisation in a more colourful way than could any chronological history.

The towns included are Kells, Downpatrick, Carrickfergus, Maynooth, Enniscorthy, Bandon, Lurgan, Ennistymon, Castlecomer, Bray, Sligo, Athlone, Dungarvan and Mullingar.

MORE IRISH COUNTRY TOWNS

Edited by
Anngret Simms and J. H. Andrews

A continuation of the first volume – the towns included in this book are Kildare, Carlingford, Bangor, Coleraine, Carrickmacross, Tullamore, Monasterevan, Athenry, Tuam, Westport, Roscrea, Cashel, Tralee, Youghal and Wexford.

BEYOND THE BLACK PIG'S DYKE

A SHORT HISTORY OF ULSTER

Art ó Broin

Beyond the Black Pig's Dyke is a concise history of Ireland's most fascinating province, from pre-history to the Republican and Loyalist ceasefires and the peace talks at the end of 1994. Drawing on the latest historical sources, it seeks to give an even-handed and accessible account of a region that has become associated with conflict but that has also made an immeasurable contribution to science, to the arts and to the development of liberal nonconformist political thought.

The geological legacy of the Ice Age was a natural barrier of drumlins and wetland between Ulster and the rest of Ireland. Early settlers supplemented nature's work with their own earthworks and the most famous of these barriers was known as the Black Pig's Dyke. In direct contrast, the Ulster planters, mainly Scots, who colonised Ulster in the cataclysmic seventeenth century, regarded the North Channel not as a boundary but as an inland sea. Part of Ireland yet separate, and with adamantine links with Britain, it is small wonder that Ulster's history has been eventful and turbulent.

THE COURSE OF IRISH HISTORY

Edited by
T.W. Moody and F. X. Martin

Though many specialist books on Irish history have appeared in the past fifty years, there have been few general works broadly narrating and interpreting the course of Irish history as a whole, in the light of new research. That is what this book set out to do; and it is a measure of its success that it is still in demand.

The first of its kind in its field, the book provides a rapid short survey, with geographical introduction, of the whole course of Ireland's history. Based on the series of television programmes first transmitted by Radio Telefis Éireann from January to June 1966, it is designed to be both popular and authoritative, concise but comprehensive, highly selective but balanced and fair-minded, critical but constructive and sympathetic. A distinctive feature is its wealth of illustrations.

The present edition is a revised and enlarged version of the original book. New material has been added, bringing the narrative to the I.R.A. ceasefire of 31 August 1994; the bibliography, chronology and index have been augmented accordingly.

THE GREAT IRISH FAMINE

Edited by
Cathal Póirtéir

This is the most wide-ranging series of essays ever published on the Great Irish Famine and will prove of lasting interest to the general reader. Leading historians, economists, geographers – from Ireland, Britain and the United States – have assembled the most up-to-date research from a wide spectrum of disciplines, including medicine, folklore and literature, to give the fullest account yet of the background and consequences of the famine. Contributors include Dr Kevin Whelan, Professor Mary Daly, Professor James Donnelly and Professor Cormac Ó Gráda.

The Great Irish Famine is the first major series of essays on the Famine to be published in Ireland for almost fifty years.